Enjoy!
D. E. Vincent
To Kathy

# CLIMAX kids, 1956

by

D. E. Vincent

authorHOUSE™

1663 LIBERTY DRIVE, SUITE 200
BLOOMINGTON, INDIANA 47403
(800) 839-8640
WWW.AUTHORHOUSE.COM

First published by AuthorHouse 09/30/04

ISBN: 1-4184-9940-4 (sc)

Printed in the United States of America
Bloomington, Indiana

This book is printed on acid-free paper.

# Chapter One

*A capricious wind blows a song along the treetops on the golden flanks of the mountain and fills a little girl's soul with the harmony of life's wonders. Then, a bittersweet discord, a sour note as one striking a wrong piano key, briefly flutters her heart, but as the child turns her face up to the blue sky, the disquietude floats away into flecks of yellow sunbeams . . .*

We sprint up the steep hill, a hill spotted with stunted spruce and pine, toward two moss rock boulders half buried in the hillside. The air is thin and chilly. Most people would have trouble breathing at this elevation, but we do not, because we're probably part mountain goats. Just now, we crane our necks to catch a glimpse of our foe.

"Here they come! See? Right over there?" Squinting hard, I point to a scraggly group of kids running through the trees below us.

"Hide quick so they can't follow us and wreck any more of our forts." My sister Becky's face looks hot and her neck sweaty under her jean jacket, as she throws herself down on a pillow of moss growing behind the sizeable rocks.

I drop down beside her and pull the ends of my scarf tighter under my chin. And then with tears in my voice I gulp out, "I'm scared of those mean kids."

"Don't be such a crybaby, Debbie," Becky says. Then she nudges my arm and points with her chin. "Look-it. They're leaving. Must have given up. Come on, let's go home for lunch."

"Okay." As I agree, the noon whistle blares shrilly.

Becky, ten, and myself, at almost eight, dash lickety-split through the woods, jumping stumps, dodging evergreen branches, leaping over rocks and boulders.

We hurry through the back door, kick off our shoes, and pile our jackets by the washer in the utility room. Washing up quickly at the kitchen sink, Becky hollers, "Mom!" And I do, too.

1

--Our mom, Celia Vincent, who grew up on a farm in southern Colorado, was more a sunflower blossom than a high-country alpine buttercup. In those days she sewed, cleaned, cooked, baked, raised kids, and saw after the needs of her husband. She worked very hard six and a half days a week "'Til my tongue is hanging out," she would say. People thought her beautiful--and she was, Coca-Cola-ad beautiful. She kept her house spotless, her kids and husband very well cared for, but she was mostly discontented with her life. Only years later did I come to understand that her life had not turned out like she thought it would, not like her childhood dreams, rather she was suppressed by the doldrums of the unfulfilled housewife of the '50s.--

Now she enters the kitchen just as my six-year-old brother, Artie, slams through the back door.

"Mom, can we have a picnic in the back yard?" he asks breathlessly.

"Oh, it's too windy," she says, glancing out the kitchen window at the clothes on the line whipping about like whirling dervishes.

"Oh, please! Please, Mom!" all three of us plead. I attempt to make my face look precious, like Mom says we are. I think Becky and Artie are trying to look like this, too.

Mom studies her children's dear faces and sighs. "Oh, all righty." She promptly wraps sandwiches and chips in waxed paper, pours milk into glass jars, and hands each of us a paper bag.

"Thanks, Mom," we remember to say.

Off I skip, laughing with my sister and brother around the clothesline stand and up an incline to the base of a car-sized boulder, which offers some protection from the wind. We sit down, our backs hugging the rock, while we savor the novelty of eating outside, windy or not. Who cares?

--The yellowish-gray boulders, like the one we sat against, were an integral part of the high-country landscape, having been blasted from the flanks of Mt. Bartlett in past decades. Mining molybdenum--or "Moly," pronounced molly—a rare metal used for strengthening steel, was the way the men at Climax, Colorado, made their living. Often miners liked to joke about the name: Moly be damned!

Even though it was first prospected and claimed by Charles Senter in 1879, Mt. Bartlett was regarded as valueless for decades, until 1900, when the gray rock outcroppings were identified as containing the rare metal. An eastern mining company, American Metals, Limited, acquired the claims, Max Schott began the mining exploration, and the era of the Climax Molybdenum Mine began. To accommodate the silver boom in Leadville, a narrow-gauge railroad was laid over Fremont Pass. It was the construction crews of the Denver, South Park, and Pacific Railroad which, upon reaching the summit of the pass, named the place "Climax."

However slow to begin because of the inhospitable locale, the camp nevertheless grew and flourished from the austere boarding houses that afforded little else than shelter from the elements, to a community rivaling only itself in quality of life. Two world wars prompted the research, development, and increase in molybdenum's monetary value, and men of vision foresaw the necessity of keeping miners content by having their families with them at their worksite.

Art Vincent, an Ohioan, was one of those who brought his family in 1948 to the mining camp, sitting at 11,320 feet high in the Rocky Mountain Mosquito Range, which straddles the Continental Divide at the precise center of the state of Colorado. Dad liked the work well enough, and moved up the ladder faster than most. In fact, only four years after starting work as a miner's helper, a "gofer"--almost the lowest job on the hill--he was promoted to a Shift Boss, a management position with a generous annual bonus. And when he retired in 1980--because people who worked at elevations of 10,000 feet or higher at that time were required by law to retire at age 60--he held the position of General Mine Foreman.

Working in the mine was fine, but the winter weather, well, that was "another thing all-to-gether," he would say. To declare that he disliked snow would be a glaring understatement, as snow meant only one thing to my dad: shoveling, shoveling, and shoveling a full nine months of the year. He said that friends coming off shift would ask those just coming through the adit, "How's the weather?" Report: "Still and clear." Translation: Still snowing and clear up to your behind. Fact: The average annual snow base in the Mosquito Range is five to six feet.—

Anyway, as I open my lunch sack, for some reason I'm thinking about the earth with salt all over it, because once my grandfather called me the salt of the earth. I don't know what that means exactly, but it does sound uniquely satisfying to me. Later I'll know what it means and the knowing will make me want to climb into my grandfather's ample lap and kiss his ruddy cheek, were he still alive. For now, I just stop thinking about salt while we eat our lunch, and after a while I recount to Artie, whose wide eyes confirm a good deal of interest, a detailed version of the morning's adventure--the chase, the hiding, and how we finally ditched our foe.

Becky says she's planning it all out in her head how we'll carry out a raid to get the things back that have been taken from our favorite fort. She tells Artie and me that we'll have to wait for the rest of the 10th Street kids to rendezvous though, those being the Priers, Brothers, Wadsworths, and Ducharmes. But this will not easily occur, I'm thinking, because of family trips, summer school, and oh, just every kind of interference with summertime fun.

My family lives at 112 10th Street, the highest street in Climax with no houses beyond ours. All of us consider it to be the greatest place in the whole wide world to live.

--During the 1930s, the powers-that-be determined that if molybdenum production was to keep up with demand, the excessive attrition rate in the work force had to be remedied. Miners simply had to be enticed to stay on longer than a few months. They put together a long-term investment by building an entire community: a hotel/boarding house, a recreation hall with a commissary, a school with a gymnasium, a hospital/clinic, a community church, apartment buildings, and hundreds of modern houses. Aside from all this, the camp boasted the highest Post Office in the country, situated in the Fremont Trading Post, which was a company store, set directly across the highway from the gatehouse to the mine. With these accommodations, miners and their families enthusiastically made Climax home. So, as the Company grew, so did the camp's community, and the amenities provided for the residents were bountiful.

The houses on White Level, among the first built in camp on streets that ran perpendicular to most of the others, were actually units of four apartments each with four rooms: kitchen, living room, bathroom and a single bedroom boasting a huge walk-in closet. As a matter of fact, my family lived in a White Level apartment during our first winter in camp- -imagine a family of five living in such a tiny place! Since housing was always at a premium in Climax, the mine's owners devised a complex system of "points" during the '50s, wherein an employee was awarded a residence based on his years of seniority with the Company, the size of his family and how young his children were. This system, however simple and straightforward at the outset, became increasingly more and more complex and political with the years. By 1956, a "new hire" with a family might have to reside in a White Level apartment until more spacious accommodations became available. Of course, there was also that breed of employee who only wanted to make a fast buck, who moved in and out of the White Level four-plexes, took no pride in his dwelling, made no commitment to the community, and scurried away the minute things got tough.--

Summertime fun includes the common game of "us against you" which kids play, and can easily occupy our attention for weeks. Our complicated battle tactics usually don't pan out, and the few times when we have actually butted heads with an adversary, the skirmishes are inconsequential, generally consisting of name-calling and taunting.

The White Level hooligans, the Finches, who hounded my sister and me this morning, have only been in camp for two months. My dad says that Mr. Finch is already pretty darned sick of the cold, damp mine, the nasty weather when he has a day off, and just about everything else about Climax, except the pay. He works on my dad's dayshift crew and talks about this stuff all the time. And, small wonder, Dad said at supper the other night, that the kids, aged four to twelve, suffer by all the moving from place to place--six times in ten years. Well, I'd say that they are tough-acting and even a bit mean-spirited and they don't mind pilfering something that isn't theirs. After all, as far as they're concerned, anything not nailed down is up for grabs, right?

On the one hand, Finch tells himself that it isn't self-indulgence which drives him, but rather that he is one who lives for the moment. Well, says Finch, who can blame him?—he's just a man searching for his niche, a comfort zone, a job that won't tax his sensibilities too much. The fact that he gives little consideration about what is good for his wife and kids is entirely beside the point, in his opinion. However, his thinking on the matter seems contradictory to my dad and me because what his entire family lacks is a social conscience.

At any rate, Becky says she's going to figure a way to get our belongings back from the Finches. She, Artie, and I, spend the afternoon waiting around for any of our friends to get home. Finally, a car drives up next door. Becky and I hurry right over and she knocks at the back door of the Priers' house. Evelyn opens the door.

"Hey, you want to help get our stuff back that those stupid White-Level-scum-of-the-earth stole? They chased Debbie and me all over this morning, trying to scare us off."

"Can't. I got to clean the kitchen and start supper before my dad gets home from work," says Evelyn, who, at twelve, is older than most of us on the street. And she definitely seems to have more everyday chores than the rest of us, although she is a time-waster; it takes her twice as long as it should to do her chores.

Evelyn's pokiness makes Becky's head sizzle up because every able-bodied kid is needed for the attack, so she bursts out, "Mom just made us Popsicles. I'm going to see if the Brothers can play." The Popsicles she goads our friend with a bit spitefully are really Kool Aide frozen in ice trays and eaten out of a piece of waxed paper.

"Who cares?" Evelyn shoots back. And she really doesn't care, which makes Becky even more irritated. My sister storms home and slams through the back screen door with me trailing behind.

That night in the bedroom we share, Becky tells me what she thinks: that she'll have to wait until morning to get everyone together; but, if she could do it alone, by heck, she would! She says she knows she'd be outnumbered, outfoxed, and outmaneuvered if she tries all by herself, though.

The next morning right after breakfast, Danny and David Prier, nine and seven, knock at the back door. I come and open it.

"Can you guys come out and play?" David asks.

"After we eat breakfast and make our beds and stuff," I tell him.

"Okay. We'll wait over at the swings."

The swings are in a small playground behind 10th Street, just up from where 11th Street starts by the boulder field. At one time, a surface maintenance crew bulldozed some boulders into a giant pile and left it right there, so when it came time to build the next street, the construction was waylaid, but finally they just built the 11th Street houses where the boulders stopped, which left this street a third the length of the others. This particular boulder pile is an especially favorite place for us to play. We have at least three secret forts hidden within it, and places like these are the reason Climax is a kids' paradise for exploring and adventure.

Five kids meet at the swings fifteen minutes later. The Prier boys and us Vincent kids decide that a simple face-to-face action plan will work best. We hike unhurriedly past 11th Street where Jacky Ducharme, Artie's best friend, hooks up with us. Marching along, this valiant troop has no doubt that justice will prevail. Across the baseball field and under a fence takes us to within a rock's throw of the Finch house. The Prier boys are notorious rock throwers and have come armed with plenty of ammo. But as soon as Becky notices this, she puts the kibosh to anything but the agreed-upon plan. She can be like an army drill sergeant when she needs to be, and she does need to take charge of this battle right now. We round the corner of the house and there before our very eyes, right where the whole world can see is our stuff from the fort--right in the middle of that front porch!

Beck pounds up the porch steps, then she turns and motions for all of us to follow her. But none of us wants to. We don't have her resolve, or her guts when it comes right down to it--me more than anybody. My stomach begins to do acrobatics, my teeth are starting up a chattering and my eyes are getting all watery. And the worst of all is that my legs have turned into wobbly gelatin, giving me an excuse for not joining my sister on the front lines.

Knock, knock, and knock! It is Mrs. Finch who comes to the door, but some scowling faces peer out from behind the window curtains.

"What?" the woman asks my sister. She isn't an oversized woman, maybe just a tad on the heavy side, and she's wearing one of those summer cotton housedresses, nothing remarkable about that, but her pointy teeth and callous voice make goose bumps pop up all over my arms and legs. Her words come out with a throaty harshness that sounds like every kind of wicked witch my imagination will conjure up.

"We've come for our stuff—it's right here on your porch," Beck says in a soft, yet mighty voice and she points right to the junked-up pile.

"No, that belongs to my kids," the woman barks. "They told me all about how they'd found some stuff off in the woods that was just left there, sorta abandoned."

"Huh-uh! They took it from our fort in the woods behind our house. It's ours, and we want it back!" Becky exclaims hotly.

I am holding my breath and my eyes remain fastened to the woman's mouth that seems to be sucking my strength down into its gaping, hideous cavern.

"It's theirs! Now, get off this property or I'll call the guards!"

"Run for your lives!" we wail, racing to the safety of our homes. Our undersized army retreats as though we're being pursued by the hounds of hell. For it is this threat above any other that terrorizes the kids in camp: We don't want the guards putting our names in any black book!

It is over. We will never see our play furniture, toys, or dishes again.

As for our enemy, who knows when they moved from Climax? Probably later in the summer. One thing's for sure--those kids never went to Max Schott School.


All week long Mom packs camping stuff for Becky because my sister is going to a Girl Scout camp for one whole week. I think Becky is very, very brave to go all by herself to a strange place even if it does promise to be the greatest adventure in the entire universe. None of us has ever been anywhere away from home without Mom and Dad.

Right after church on Sunday, Dad piles all my sister's camp stuff into the trunk and then it's time to leave for Salida and the Mt. Shavano Girl Scout Camp.

"Hey, Becky, how's come you need a fishing pole when you've never even ever been fishing?" I ask after we've been driving for a while and I've had time to ponder a few things.

"Because a fishing pole was on my list of stuff to bring with me and anyway, they're going to teach me how. I'll catch some fish and bring some home, too," she tells me, using her standard, overconfident-sounding tone.

"Oh." Leaning over the seat and touching my mom's soft, velvety cheek, I ask, "Mom, do I like to eat fish?"

"You don't like to eat fish any more than you like to eat anything, Debbie," she answers with a sigh.

And that is accurate. Sometimes I hide my sandwich in a napkin and throw it behind the washing machine when no one's looking. Eating is not my best thing. I can hold peas in my mouth for a long, long time without squishing a single one and then I just wait for an opportunity to spit them into the garbage after everyone's done with dinner.

The drive down is tedious because first we go through Leadville and this section of the highway is so familiar that it offers very little of interest. The next twenty miles is better as the road follows the Arkansas River on one side and farmlands on the other. Sheep and cows graze lazily in lush green fields just this side of the small town of Buena Vista and I become drugged by the quietude and fall sound asleep, so I miss seeing the small city of Salida altogether. When I wake up, Dad is driving cautiously up a mountain dirt road to the camp.

It has begun to rain in earnest, which means Artie and I have to stay in the car while Dad unloads Becky's stuff from the trunk. My brother and I scrunch our faces against the car window, so we can watch where Becky and some other girls are heading. But we lose sight of them as they round the corner of a large, wood-sided building where Mom and Dad have taken my sister's stuff. And before I know it my parents climb right back into the car and we pull away.

"Mom, is it time to leave Becky here? I wanted to tell her goodbye, but I didn't even get to." I am astonished and unhappy and my voice sounds impressively indignant to my ears.

But Mom is blowing her nose and her head is bent forward. She doesn't answer me.

"Dad, how come I didn't even get to tell Becky goodbye or wave or anything?"

"Look here," he says in a very gentle, whispery voice, "you people have never been away from home before. So this is kind of hard on your mother and me."

Well, on Tuesday, Becky calls us on the telephone and says that she does not want to stay at the camp and that we'd just better come back down there and get her. On Wednesday, Dad takes the day off and we drive all the way back down to Salida to collect her home.

As Dad drives back up the dirt road to the camp, Becky is sitting on the steps of the main lodge with all her camping gear piled beside her.

On the way home, I keep up a constant barrage of questions about the Girl Scout Camp--I myself am all but bursting with curiosity. However, my sister chooses to regale us with stories describing the counselors and the other campers, and she moves quickly from one person to the next so that my questions remain unanswered. Becky finally tells us that she does not want to talk about the camp, and so she does not.

--Many years later, I experience homesickness firsthand, and I remembered my sister's insistence to push it away; it helped her pretend that none of it had happened. She never did like to admit to weakness.—

All in all, the best part of the drive home is that she teaches my brother and me every song that she'd learned sitting around the campfire at night. "High on a mountain ledge I built my wigwam. Close to the water's edge, silent and still. Blue lake and mountain shore, I will return once more. Boom ditty ah da! Boom ditty ah da! Booooom!" One of us has to make drum noises to maintain a beat as we sing. Becky easily teaches us the words to two more songs, "In a Cabin in the Woods," and "Oh, She Sailed Away," that we enjoy because of the hand motions that go along with them. And because she is a very adept teacher, we learn them promptly.

# Chapter Two

*A little hard work never hurts anyone, and if you want something bad enough you have to be willing to work hard for it . . . a sagacious idiom meant to aid the young along life's thoroughfares. Seemingly, children can easily change work into games, and then again, sometimes fun can be very hard work, indeed. Satisfied is the young child who keeps at her task to the bitter end.*

Summer thundershowers keep everyone close to home for a week; but, as soon as the weather clears, eight kids collect over by the boulder field. Jimmy Ducharme, who is eight and in my grade, gets everyone excited and agitated right away. He has dark brown hair, brown eyes and an impish grin on his round, freckled face.

"Remember those flowers we took up to Phillipson's grave? Somebody's been there and tore everything all apart!" Jimmy reports waving his arms around.

--Brainerd F. Phillipson was one of the early developers of Climax Molybdenum Company and his ashes were buried above the portal of the Phillipson Tunnel on Mt. Bartlett in the spring of 1930. Time and the relentless nature of the high-altitude elements were actually Jimmy's vandals. Very near the time of this narrative, in 1955, Phillipson's widow came to Climax for a brief memorial service at the gravesite after which his remains were removed and taken back East.—

"Huh! How do you know? Did you see?" Becky asks, dropping the stick she's been scratching in the dirt with.

"Paulie said, and he knows!" Paulie is Jimmy's junior high school brother, who wants to play on the Blue Devil's basketball team, and as such, he has all the authority needed to make believers of us.

Hence, a plan is put into action to snatch this opportunity to set a wrong to right by immediately rushing up and over the hogback and beyond to the gravesite.

It's around nine in the morning when we begin the steep uphill climb through the conifer and spruce. Soon we sight our first point of reference: the water tanks.

--A high, chain-link fence surrounded the two tanks, notification enough for all to stay clear. This tanked water was used to pump down into the mine for several reasons. First, there were two-inch lines of pipe that pumped in purified water to guarantee that the concrete, used for shoring up tunnels, would set properly. The miners in the stopes used water from one-inch pipes attached to hoses for cooling their drill bits. Compressors used water as a coolant for air for the miners underground. Because the water inside the mine was full of contaminates, such as arsenic and lead, signs were posted all over the mine telling people not to drink the water coming from pipes under any circumstances. Miners carried their drinking water in with them in pint bottles. So: Trespassers Beware! --

"Whew! Let's rest here a minute," Patrick Wadsworth, ten, suggests, as he wipes his sweat-streaked face with the tattered, grimy sleeve of a shirt he's worn for the past three days. His unruly light brown hair wisps around his face. He has eight brothers and sisters, three older than he is, and that's got to be a lot of clothes washing. But, he says he always likes to wear his favorite shirt, no matter.

A rest sounds fine to all of us; it has taken us a good chunk of time to trek along this far.

"Hey, you guys! Look way, way down there. See our houses?" Jimmy asks, as he stretches his arm and points straight down the hillside.

"Oh, yeah, and look-it, there's the train trestle and some cars waiting for the train to cross over. See?" Artie says with a pleased grin.

"What if the train comes off the tracks and crashes down on the cars? Ker-splat!" Jacky, who's a mirror image of Jimmy, says, mostly to Joe and Artie. All three of them start to giggle and horse around, wrestling and making loud car/train crashing noises.

And now every single one of us takes a turn to point out something or other. We can sure see a whole bunch of stuff going on all over camp when we're up high like now.

"Come on, giddy-up, you guys, or we'll never get to the grave," Patrick says.

We start out again.

None of us has thought to bring water along; we don't really need to because of all the unspoiled creeks running down from snowfields, but the first of these creeks is over the hogback, which is a good half hour away. We are now driven onward by our thirst.

In due time, the bigger kids reach the ridgeline and sit down to wait for us stragglers to catch up. No talking, just gazing at God's creation, which surrounds the group in any direction they might choose to look. A brisk breeze dries up the sweat on their necks and faces in no time at this elevation.

--Azure skies of gem-like brilliance, dotted with high, puffy clouds look innocent and to the novice pose no immediate threat. However, high-country mountain storms can develop with no warning and can turn into deadly thunder and lightning storms in minutes. Years later, as adults, my friends and I were caught twice by storms while climbing Colorado 14'ers. Once, when climbing a "double"--reaching two peaks on a single climb--Harvard and Columbia in the Collegiate Range, we simply ran out of time and were forced to crawl off the summit of Columbia on our bellies as the lightning crackled around us. And again, on a difficult assent of Mt. Bierstadt in the Front Range, after having negotiated a forbidding saw-toothed ridge from Mt. Evans that cost us precious time, we had to move stealthily from the summit on all fours, keeping our bodies below the boulders to avoid the lightening from the sudden, unexpected storm.—

"Come on, you guys, hurry up!" Jimmy Ducharme shouts down to us littler kids, our heads just now bobbing up and down through the piney scrub.

"We're coming, wait up!" This from Artie, who is hindered by a large walking stick he has come across. He is using it as a make-believe machete, and lots of swishing sounds are necessary as he walks along. Jacky follows close behind him because he is an important explorer being led by Tarzan through the jungle to a meeting with the tribe's bloodthirsty leader. The two have some prisoners dragging behind, namely Joe Wadsworth, six years old, David Prier, and me.

Ten minutes brings us to the top of the ridge where Jimmy, Patrick, and Becky are sprawled out on the summer-soft tundra.

"About time, you morons! Let's go!" Jimmy says, mildly contemptuous.

"What? We just got here!" his little brother, Jacky, complains. "Hey, you guys want some raisins? You can have the rest, if you don't start off without us." He pulls a large, badly crushed box out of his jacket pocket and holds it up for inspection.

The three bigger kids agree and quickly divvy up the snack, while we slowpokes sit down on some moss rocks and relax our worn-out selves.

"Before we get to the grave's fence, let's stop and wait for everybody to catch up just in case there's spies around watching. Okay?" David suggests hopefully, looking at the older kids.

Okay everyone agrees, and we set off once more. We drop off the side of the hogback and into some willows. The whole area is spongy with snowfield runoff. Each of us stoops in turn to drink from a trickle of spring water flowing over mossy-green rocks. Nothing in the world could taste as sweet and refreshing as this. With our thirst quenched, we take time to pick some white alpine lilies to take along to the gravesite.

--I've thought back to this time often, again while climbing the Colorado 14-ers. We always carry drinking water with us because of the threat of *giardia*, a parasitic bacteria sometimes found in mountain streams, which causes stomach cramps, diarrhea and misery. I always wonder how it was that none of us were ever stricken with it when we lived in Climax. The mountain goats and sheep, the marmots and picas that drank from streams and carried the bacteria were surely as plentiful then as today. There was talk circulating around the Climax kids that polio was transmitted by drinking water from any source other than kitchen taps. Although this did put a scare into us, we soon forgot all about polio as we continued along our happy-go-lucky way of life.—

Onward we tramp and presently come to some more fields of wild flowers, which turn the high, alpine meadow into swirls of rainbows.

Indian paintbrush, columbine and daisies are abundant, so we pick bouquets to add to the lilies already wilting in our grubby hands.

Just visible at the far end of the meadow is a wrought-iron fence clearly in need of a coat of paint. We sprint to the gate of the enclosure and read the plaque with a reverence given to such places difficult to reach, and also a wonderment that this person could have lived so long ago. The inscription reads: IN LOV MEMOR OF B.F. PHILLIPSON, DIED 1930 The rest has been eaten away by time and the elements. The latch on the gate is rusted and warped out of shape so Patrick and Jimmy pull on it with all their might until it creaks outward eight inches on near useless hinges. Everyone is able to squeeze through the opening and then we place our flower offerings beside the stone marker before stepping back to the fence. We make a thorough going-over of the place, looking for any signs of wrongdoing. Finally, noting no obvious trespassers have been in there, Becky shoots a telling look in Jimmy's direction and I'm sure from the look in her eyes that warnings from Paulie Ducharme will never again figure into our future plans.

Hiking back is twice as fast, especially after we top the ridge. When we get back to the water tanks, we decide to walk on a gravelly road, actually more of a track, used by service vehicles. The slope is very steep and we don't have sure footing like we would have if we'd taken a shortcut through the woods. Just down from the tanks, the road curves and as we round the bend we freeze in mid-stride. The most amazing sight greets us on the edge of that road: a gigantic tractor tire! We run around it in a near frenzy of supposing.

Everyone prattles on at the same time.

"Who left it here?"

"How's come it was abandoned?"

"Could it possibly be free ?"

"Do we dare consider moving it?"

The Stork Level whistle terminates our gaiety and sends us flying down the road to our homes. Before we part we promise to meet again immediately after lunch.

In less than thirty minutes we have re-grouped by the boulder field, although we are now only six because the Wadsworth boys have to take care of their younger brothers and sisters for the rest of the afternoon.

"I don't think it's for free. Maybe we better just leave it alone," I contribute, fiddling with my jacket buttons.

"Shut up, scaredy cat," Jimmy hisses.

"You shut up, stupid head! Leave my sister alone or I'll--" Becky fires back at him.

Jimmy backs down from the unspoken threat for the time being, as there are much more important dealings facing us. "Look, we need to get back up there right now before anyone else finds it," he says.

"Yeah, let's go!" everyone quickly agrees.

So back up the mountain we scurry. The tractor tire is right where we'd last seen it. We whoop for joy, touching, nudging, and darned near worshipping the abandoned tire. It is so big that I can just manage to rest my chin on it. Finally, we scramble atop it to catch our breath and contemplate the tire's zillions of uses; and, because of the way we find ourselves sitting on it, a flash of inspiration strikes! No one is able to say for certain who initially came up with the idea, but "Yes! Yes! Yes!" we shout.

Our fearsome activity begins by first figuring out how to get the tire unstuck from its bed of dirt and grasses. Tools will be needed, that's for sure. Artie, Jacky, and David, are sent to gather anything useful from their dads' caches. The rest of us announce that we will continue at the task facing us. While the boys are gone we scrape, dig, and scratch with steady resolve for the good part of an hour with almost no results to show for our efforts. Finally, we sit down to rest.

"This is too hard! Where are those boys, anyway?" Becky grumbles, wiping her face with her red plaid cotton shirttail.

"Yeah. This stupid thing is stuck like stink on stink," Jimmy says, his face scrunched into a scowl, as he drapes himself over the tire.

"I'm thirsty. I wish we had some Kool Aide. It's too hot for this kind of hard work," I moan, propping myself against the side of the tire next to my sister.

Before we've waited too much longer, we hear voices coming from the woods below us, but long minutes pass before we actually see the boys appear from the trees.

I run down to meet them.

"Jeepers, creepers! Where have you guys been, anyway? We coulda had this out by now, if you weren't so gosh-darned slow!" a glum Jimmy greets them.

"Hey! Look it what we got!" the smaller kids gush noisily, ignoring the grudging welcome. They proudly display two tire irons, a hammer, three screwdrivers, and a handful of nails. Danny Prier is with them now; he'd been in a summer school session in the morning.

"What's the hammer for? Pounding on knuckleheads?" Jimmy scoffs.

"Quit being such a brat all the time, Jimmy. Let's get going, you guys," Becky says, grabbing one of the tire irons.

We do. As the afternoon wears on, we manage to clear most of the hard-packed earth from all around the bottom of the tire. Every so often we try to budge it, with no success.

Shadows are getting longer and a hazy quiet begins to blanket the surrounding woods. There is a particular feel to the air that speaks to us in soft, hushed ways. The birds and other critters know when it is time to call it a day.

And as if on cue, the Phillipson Level whistle sounds out shrilly. We all concede that for this day the work will have to cease. Seven filthy, exhausted kids angle down through the woods to supper as quickly as possible. As we trudge wearily along we worry that some lucky no-account kids might happen across our valuable find. But we know we will just have to hope against hope and pray for the dawn to make a hasty showing so that we can get back to the treasure.

At eight o'clock the following morning, we gobble down our breakfast as fast as we can swallow. Mom is singing "Oh, What a Beautiful Morning!" But she stops to ask what our big hurry is.

"We found a giant tractor tire over by the tanks, Mom!" Artie blurts. "It's really, really neat! But we have to hurry before someone else finds it."

Her face shows us that she enjoys hearing about our adventures and she often says that it pleases her that we have such a good time, and that we are filled with such an unlimited joy of life in this mining camp. "Well, just stay out of trouble," she warns us, smiling, and then she goes on singing.

"Mom, can we take some water up there, please?" Becky asks, thinking back to the previous afternoon. As it turns out, she's the only one who did think about water.

Mom had been cleaning out the Fridge the day before, and happens to have a large jar handy. "Sure. Here's an empty mayonnaise jar you can fill with water. Just don't break it and hurt yourselves."

"Thanks, Mom," Becky says as she fills the jar at the sink. Cradling it in her arm, she dashes away.

"'Bye, Mom!" Artie calls on his way out the back screen door.

I hug her legs and say, "I love you! 'Bye! See you at lunchtime!"

Danny and David Prier race out their back door and jog with us over to the boulder field. We climb to the top of the pile so that we can see over to 11th Street and watch for the Ducharmes. After just a few minutes the five of us can wait no longer; we are too eager to get back up to our most wonderful discovery.

"I'm going to go get them. Wait, okay?" Artie says.

"No. We're not waiting; we've got to get up there right now. You guys can meet us," Becky tells him.

"Okay. We'll hurry up. See you in a minute." He runs off.

It takes us no time at all to climb back up to the tractor tire. We each hold our breath before stepping from the woods. However, we have undershot the target and don't immediately see it on the service road.

"Oh, no! It's gone!" I whisper, my hands flying to my mouth.

"No! It can't be. It just can't be," Becky mutters, still cradling the water jar in her arm like it's a little baby.

Danny and David start to jog up an especially steep rise in the road. Becky and I follow right on their heels. Everyone is breathing laboriously as we round a curve and stop dead still.

"Yea!! Hooray!" We whoop and holler as we scamper the last dozen yards to our prize.

The evening before no one had given a thought to our dads' tools. But as luck would have it, the tools lay strewn all over the area where we'd left them. We all start in digging with energetic eagerness. In time, a four-inch ditch completely surrounds the tire.

Finally, Becky, Danny, David, and I, get ready to push mightily against one side, as Danny counts down, "Five, four, three, two, one, push! Again!

Give it everything you got! Ready? Five, four, three, two, one, go!" A third time. Then a fourth.

Nothing. Not one teensy bit of give from the tire. It seems that old Mother Earth is playing a cruel game of tug-o'-war. We drop to the mostly rocky ground worn out and pitiful and drink from the water jar that has been resting against a nearby tree.

"Hey, you guys! Where are you?" comes a yell from down in the woods.

"We're way up here! Keep walking!" Becky calls out, hands cupped around her mouth.

As the Ducharme boys and Artie approach us weary workers, David asks, "What took you guys so dang long?"

"Yeah! We need help. We can't get this thing to budge an inch," Danny says, jumping to his feet.

"Yeah! We need help," I echo, as I stand up and brush off the seat of my pants.

"Copycat! Copycat! You can't even catch a rat!" Jimmy sing-songs at me, dancing around like a loony marionette.

"Shut up!" Becky snaps. "Anyway, you're so ignorant! That's not even the way it goes!"

"Who cares?" he cracks back.

"If you don't watch it, Jimmy Ducharme, you're not even going to get to be part owner of this tractor tire!" she explodes. And she probably thinks to herself, like I do, how sick and tired she is of him, because he thinks he is so smart just 'cause his brother is almost in high school. Big deal.

"Oh, yeah? Says who, you big baboon?"

"Come on, you guys! We have to get this thing moved sometime, you know," Danny cuts in.

So one kind of battle ends for the time being, giving over to the battle with the tire. Over the course of days that it takes us 10th Street kids to wrestle the tractor tire down the mountainside, many scuffles and arguments keep us tangled together, as we thrash about day after day grappling with the tire's bulk and weight. That big old thing is awkward and tricky every time we get our hands on it. See, every kid gets on one side and lifts until the tire's standing on end so we can roll it. But if, say, a large rock or rut is in the direct path while we have the tire balanced and rolling between us--ka boom, bam!--down it goes, clouds of dirt and pine needles rising. Or when there's not enough kid-power, very little moving forward is made, only maybe a yard or two. And oddly, none of us has given a single thought about the chance of our tire being stolen away in the night since we first found it. Huh! Fat chance!

Five and a half days of backbreaking, sweat-and-dirt-filled work (not counting Sunday morning when most us have to go to church) is how long it takes us to move the tire from its original resting place below the tanks to its new home. Not its final address, just near the back yards of the 10th Street houses. At this point in time a meeting is called to order. Anyone who wants to is given a chance to stake a claim to have his own yard as the place for the tire. However, parent after parent nixes the idea of this unsightly prize being placed on their property. Until at last Becky, Artie, and I, are able to wear down our mom, and she reluctantly agrees to it. And since the Priers' parents don't raise much of an objection, the problem is solved. The tractor tire comes to a "final" resting place between the two houses.

The best part of all is the ingenious use of this tire that from its first discovery has so thrilled our group of kids. Ours will be the only wading pool in all of Climax! And, only the owners will have use of it – owners being anyone who has had a hand, great or small, in moving the tire.

Of course, if any of us admitted to the truth, we can only endure keeping our feet submerged for a few brief minutes at a time, since the sun cannot warm the water sufficiently, and it would be as pleasing to stick our bare feet into the middle of a melting snow bank! I try it most often, I think, but most of the time I just squat on the edge with my feet up, daydreaming.

The tractor tire ends up being a hot political device. To us, politics are involved in any random disagreement over the outcome of the games that we play. Bargaining and negotiating work at times, but when push comes to shove the tire often becomes the trump card.

For instance, if the trouble becomes a big enough deal between the Priers and us and an agreement cannot be reached, Artie, Becky, and I talk the 10th Street kids into moving the wading pool to the other side of our house between us and the Brothers, making the Brothers kids full owners, even though the Brothers had been on a vacation trip during the time that all this happens. Politics! As things turn out, we move the darn thing twice. Once because my dad puts our canvas camping tent up in the back yard and the Priers try to make up the rules about how it will be put to use. And again when the Brothers get too selfish with the tire, calling it their very own property, and all. Pant! Grunt! Shove! Push!

# Chapter Three

*The winding road comes to a fork and the trail to the left appears to have a sinister nature about it, but at the same time, a tantalizing scent of the never-experienced wafts from without its hazy corridors. The little girl knows right from wrong and she also knows how good it feels when she chooses to do the right thing. So, why must the choosing be so problematical at times?*

A favorite area for us 10th Street kids to play is up in the woods not too far from the water tanks in the broken-down trees.

--Sometime in the early days of Climax's development, a couple acres of trees had been cut down for one reason or another, possibly to make room for the water tanks. Another good possibility would be that the trees came from the rough road that was built for Company vehicle usage: The water tanks had to be inspected regularly, because the water had to be tested for acceptable levels of lead and arsenic contamination. At any rate, the cut trees were subsequently bulldozed into an admirable pile covering a quarter of an acre, more or less, and left there to rot. Also, it might be noted here that pieces of wood occasionally found a way into the mine workings. Imagine all the wood mixed in with the ore when the mine became an open-pit mining operation during the '70s.--

Well! This paradise is a veritable wonderland for me, and for that matter, any kid with even an ounce of imagination. Games are played, wars are waged, forts are built, and on and on, for days on end. It isn't only us 10th Street kids who play here, by any means. Practically every kid in camp knows about the area, but we frequent it more often because of its proximity to our homes. In fact, we are so familiar with the area that we have names for certain trees and/or groups of trees, for examples: the Bucking Bronco, the Genie's Secret Cave Entrance, the Pirate's Den, Tarzan's Tree House, and the Circus Tight Wire, just to name a few.

Today, Artie, Jacky, and Joe Wadsworth have a plan to go up to the broken-down trees to work on their fort. But Artie had admitted to Dad last night that he was the one who had taken tools from the garage, and so he promised to put them back before he did anything else today. And now he corners me in the back yard. I am playing with dolls under the clothesline stand, my perfect pint-sized playhouse.

--Dad had built this structure so that Mom could stand above the snow bank to hang out clothes on sunny winter days. The platform was six feet from the ground, anchored on two-by-four stilts, and had stairs snug against the back door porch. The clotheslines were secured onto a metal pole that poked up through the platform, and were rigged to a pulley that was attached to the trunk of a stout evergreen about sixty yards uphill from the house. This ingenious system worked quite well to keep clothes from dragging in the snow. During the '30s and '40s, before the Company had constructed many of the office buildings, houses, and apartment buildings, women were known to hang clothes out of their upstairs windows on clotheslines stretched to a tree top. Also of note, during those early days, households commonly used what they called "Okie iceboxes" which were wooden crates secured outside the kitchen window and used to store food that required refrigeration. By any account, families living in Climax during the decades of the '30s, '40s, and '50s were frequently driven to be inventive and resourceful--it came with the territory.—

"Hey, Deb! Will you go up where we left Dad's tools and bring them back? If you do, you can come to the broken-down trees with me and Jacky and Joe."

Well, I don't really relish the idea of retrieving those darn tools all by myself, not at all--but I *do* badly want to wander around in the broken-down trees. So . . . "Okay. Hey, I have an idea! You guys can hike up the road with me and I'll lug the tools back here. Then I can just hustle and join up with you, okay?"

Artie cheerfully agrees, and rushes off to collect his friends. Together we lope and lark through the woods like playful fawns out for a morning caper. Once at our destination, we parade from the trees onto the road and it takes only a moment to sort Dad's tools from the others lying about. My brother arranges them into my outstretched arms, and then the trio sallies forth with no further ado. I scoot back home, deliver the tools to the garage, and head back up through the woods.

When I arrive at the broken-down trees, I stand stone still as a plaster statue and listen for voices, but . . . silence. My heart is pounding in my chest and I have a stitch in my side from running and hurrying so fast. I lean against the Bucking Bronco for a minute to catch my breath and scope out the area. I strain, listening for the boys' voices again, but all I hear are summer sounds: blue jays scolding me, breezes whispering in the trees, and the sun warming everything, all filling me with purest contentment.

"Hmm," I wonder aloud, "where are those guys?" I straddle the Bucking Bronco and take pleasure in the scratchiness of the bark and the smell of sap that I've brought to the surface of the uprooted tree, with its largest end wedged between others in the massed mound. Oh! In the blink of an eye, I am riding into the world of Roy Rogers and Dale Evans. We are looking for the bandits who got away with the miners' payroll. "Giddy-up, Ol' Black! They're headin' for their hideout in the canyon!" Roy and Dale are just ahead. I get Ol' Black to gallop along pretty fast, but then he tuckers out and we lose sight of the couple.

After awhile I'm riding on a stagecoach pretending to be Calamity Jane, and so I sing a song from a movie I'd just seen this summer, "Oh, the Deadwood Stage is a-coming along, I know. Whip crack away, whip crack away, whip crack away!" at the top of my lungs. Instantly I am pitched back to the real world at the boisterous approach of Artie, Jacky, and Joe. Pulling hard on the reins I say, "Whoa, Ol' Black." And after patting his flanks, I jump down to the ground and join them.

"Come on, Deb," Artie says, as he grasps my arm. "We're playing at Tarzan's Tree House. We're jungle explorers looking for gold."

"You can pretend you're lost, and we'll find you," Joe adds, and Jacky nods his approval. All three have dirt-streaked faces and smell earthy.

"Why are you looking for gold, if it's a jungle?" I ask, as we gingerly make our way across a precarious section of downed trees.

"'Cause we're pretending there's a lost gold mine from a treasure map we found." Joe squats like a chipmunk on a scrawny tree and pulls out a dirty piece of a magazine cover from his pocket, which he stretches out for me to see. "Here, look-it."

Crrrack! Down Joe drops, leaving the rest of us to gape open-mouthed at the void he'd just created. Swirls of dust and debris almost choke us. We scramble to the edge of the hole and peer down into the dust-filled dimness. We can barely manage to stifle our giggles as we spot him down there on his behind probably no more than five feet or so.

"Help me out!" Joe is bawling his eyes out.

"Don't worry! We'll get you out," Jacky says, with an overblown air of self-importance. "Wait. We need a long stick to hand down to you."

"Hurry up, I'm bleeding to death and my leg's broke in two!" poor Joe whimpers.

We hurriedly explore the adjacent area, ultimately finding a good, stout branch, and rush back to carry out the rescue. We pass the branch down to Joe and attempt to direct him as to his part of the operation. He is blubbering so much, though, that eventually Artie and I climb down into the cavity and sort of boost him up to where Jacky can clutch onto his wrists. And then my brother and I carve out some toeholds with a sharp rock, so that we can gain purchase of the wall and shimmy back into the sunshine, where we take a studied look at Joe's imagined injuries but find them sorely lacking in severity. He wipes his snotty face on his shirtsleeve, as none of us ever seems to have a tissue at hand, and tries to get himself composed.

The treasure map is gone, and we kind of lose enthusiasm for finding gold. We're also beginning to feel hunger gnawing at our bellies, but Jacky remembers that he's brought along some raisins to share.

"Your mom sure likes to get raisins a lot, huh, Jacky?" I point out needlessly, taking a fistful.

"I guess," he mumbles, stuffing the dried fruit into his mouth.

"Hey, lets pretend we're in a war and we have to be the ambulance guys," Artie says, thinking this would be awfully fun. But Joe, still smarting from his ignominious fall, doesn't think it would be, especially.

"Hey, you guys! Follow me!" I cry, hoping my enthusiasm will act as a magnet and draw them along. I want to check on the condition of the Genie's Secret Cave Entrance. At the end of last summer we had left an old army blanket inside the cave, along with an authentic oil lantern supplied by the Ducharmes. Our friends' dad, Paul Ducharme, had been a POW in Germany during WWII and his boys always supply us with

Army surplus booty. Not that one has much to do with the other, but we always make the connection, nevertheless.

Off we charge to the perimeter of the area closest to the water tanks. We scout around until eventually I spot the marker, a U-shaped log that is really two trees somehow twisted around one another.

"Here it is! Come on!" I call out.

We creep stealthily along on all fours into the dank dimness underneath the broken-down trees, coughing on the tree dust and dirt that we have stirred into clouds. Our forward progress is gradual; numerous pointy branches scratch and poke at us from all directions. A steady chatter about which way to proceed keeps each of us wondering whether or not the place still exists. At last, as luck would have it, we stumble upon the cave purely by accident, and find the space to be pretty much as we remembered from the previous summer.

"Phewy! Look-it this army blanket--holes and tears all over it," Jacky says, holding it out for our inspection. The rest of us scrunch up our faces and cover our noses.

"Yuck! It stinks like a darn skunk!" I gasp, pinching my nose forcefully, although I've never actually smelled a skunk. We shuffle and scoot around in the cramped space, trying to sit without someone's elbows or knees in our faces. It is a really undersized cave.

"Here's the lantern," Joe says, and as he lifts the rusty relic a half-empty pack of cigarettes falls to the ground by his feet.

"Hey, what's that?"

"Let me see!"

Four sets of eyes widen incredulously as the realization sinks in about what the tattered, crushed pack contains.

Jacky shakes out the contents onto a corner of the blanket and counts audibly, "Six, seven, eight! Whoa ho! Eight cigarettes!"

Well, a palpable buzz saturates the air as we imagine the unimaginable.

I remember something that had taken place the first week of summer vacation: One evening after supper, Dad told us to remain at the kitchen table as he had recently been made aware of a situation via the mine's widespread gossip network, saying that he had it on best authority that the Prier boys had been caught smoking cigarettes, and this on more than one occasion. He continued his sermon by stating that under no circumstances should any of us be with Danny and David if the two happened to have cigarettes in their possession. He concluded with the edict that the consequences would be dire if this order was disobeyed. We nodded our heads solemnly, and vowed without guile that we could be trusted completely. And we sincerely believed that we could be.

Oh, what a wicked web Fate weaves!

The noon whistle! Out of the dead tree cave we hasten, crawling backward twice as fast as when we entered, leaving our dreadful discovery behind. Or so I think!

After lunch we have to go with Mom and Dad to Leadville, thirteen miles down a winding two-lane highway, for a visit to our dentist, Dr. Rose, and to buy groceries at the Safeway store. So, it isn't until the next day that I see my young life flash before my eyes.

I am playing house in our fort playhouse, which the Finch kids had earlier stripped of furnishings, with Becky, Evelyn Prier, and Ava Lou and Bonnie Brothers. We are busy sweeping the pine needles from the floor, using tree branch brooms. Later, we pretend that the fruits of the forest are real food products: kinnikinic is salad and chunks of wood from rotted-out evergreen trees is meat. However, our supply of meat is used up at the moment, so I offer to go off to the woods to find some. Uphill about five minutes away, I come across a fallen spruce with its trunk busted open. Oh, what a treasure find! I bend to my task--the wood we need has to be in a precise state of rottenness, moist to the touch, reddish in color, pungent smelling, and then it can be broken into various sizes to yield roasts, steaks, and hamburger meat. I am just stacking my booty into my shirtfront when I first hear and then see Artie, Joe, and Jacky galloping toward me.

"Hey, Debbie, wait up!" Artie calls. His sheepish expression tells me something untoward is in the wind.

"What? We're playing house. I have to hurry back over there," I tell them as they skid to a halt.

"Look-it what we got," Joe says, pulling the forbidden object from his jacket pocket.

The "it" is in a wrinkled, yellowed bit of newspaper.

"Let me see." I peep inside. It is the pack of cigarettes from the Genie's Secret Cave Entrance. "Uh-oh! You guys are going to get in trouble! Artie, I'm telling on you!"

"Come on, Debbie! Don't tell," each boy begs ardently, crowding and nudging against me, acting like an agitated gaggle of geese.

"Quit your pushing! Just what do you think you're going to do with them, anyway?" I demand, searching each face suspiciously.

"Nothing."

"I have to go," I say, turning my back on the trio with self-righteous scorn, and trot off in the direction of our playhouse.

"Better not tell!" they bellow as I shoot away through the woods. Back among my friends, though, a sense of impending doom is squirming around my insides. I must discover what my brother and his friends intend to do.

"I have to go to the bathroom really bad," I fib to the girls. "I'll be right back, okay?"

Of course I don't go home, though. Instead I ferret around in the woods, determined to flush the boys from their foxhole. All the way to the swings. Nope. Then over to the boulder field. No, not here either. I scale the rocks to gain a vantage point on the highest boulder, and like the bounty hunter in *Texas Ranger*, I turn in a full circle, squinting, searching. At last I catch sight of them heading to the Prier's back yard, so I hightail it over there as fast as my stick legs can sprint.

Danny and David Prier--just like Dad warned us--are showing off a box of matches to Artie, Joe, and Jacky just as I get within earshot. As soon as they see me, they shun me.

"Get out of here, traitor!" And shoo me away, like a noisome fly.

I loathe being called a spy--this is excessive and unmerited. After all, have I spoken a single word to anyone, yet? Had I felt like it, I most certainly could have told my friends at our playhouse, I point out.

"Let me come with you guys," I implore, my composure and pride leaking into tears. I ache with an urgency to keep my little brother out of harm's way, if I can. At least, I tell myself, he'll have a better chance if I'm with him. I know deep in my heart of hearts that they plan to try smoking those devil cigarettes. The ultimate danger is being caught in the act, not the act itself. This distorted logic keeps nudging my subconscious.

The boys put their heads together and argue my trustworthiness. I kick at a stone with the toe of my sneaker and peep at them as they whisper, thick as thieves. The world is still and holding its breath as I wait, not a breeze nor the stir of a flying insect disturbs the air.

"Let's give her a chance," Artie sighs in resignation, knowing I am his trusted ally when push comes to shove.

"Yeah, but she said she'd tell, remember?" Jacky recaps.

"She's my sister and she won't tell. She hardly ever tells on me unless I make her mad about something," Artie reasons.

More arguing ensues.

"Aw, let her stay, I guess," the boys finally stingily agree. But first I must swear my allegiance. You know, like to the flag.

"Cross my heart and hope to die, a thousand needles in my eye."

Whoopee! My heart leaps joyfully at being granted this dubious honor. But a mere moment later I am covered with a cloak of guilt, sweat seeps from my pores, prickling my face, and cobwebs cloud my mind. My fickle heart, a moment before swollen with elation, now rumbles with the gloominess that portends a dreadful storm.

Off we caper to a secreted den in the woods like a family of foxes intent upon a hen house attack. Even before anything happens, in my mind the judge and jury have already passed sentence and we are doomed. No heat can warm the pessimism that permeates me.

We crouch on the ground in a compact circle of conspiracy. Each kid is anticipating an epiphany, an up-close and personal revelation via the wanton undertaking, with the exception of the veteran Prier boys, and me, a cowardly, self-convicted criminal.

David's fingers scratch a match on the side of the box. The stench of sulfur attacks my nose and sends me into a sneezing fit, caused by jitters more than anything. The match doesn't light. Boy, oh, boy! He tries another. Sphitt. This one's a dud, too. I suck in my breath and hold onto it. But, the third match flames and Danny is ready with a cigarette between his lips, and he then leans close to the tiny flame and puffs as if his life depends upon it. Smoke curls out of his mouth as he hands the thing to Joe. Puff. Puff. The cigarette changes hands quickly, until it's Artie's turn to have a go. He exchanges a furtive look with me and raises his eyebrows up and down--I know that look--then he takes the cigarette to his sweet, very young lips. Puff.

Each of them, Joe, Jacky, and my brother, cough and roll around, holding their stomachs. Tears spring to my eyes. I'm heartsick from my hair to my toes. I don't even need to draw the smoke into my mouth to suffer what the boys are feeling. Each boy's puff swirls in my head and leaves me feeling groggy and green around the gills. I am guilty by association.

The noon whistle alarms us and we stagger home to lunch.

Needless to say, Artie and I have little appetite for peanut butter and jelly sandwiches, but we feign hunger for the sake of hiding our transgression.

Later on in mid-afternoon, we rush out to our back yard as the whistle siren wails out an alarm. Presently we see the paddy wagon/fire truck careening through the trees, and we sprint our fastest to follow the truck to its destination. Suddenly we see that a pine tree is engulfed in flames in close proximity to the boulder field! Naturally as we watch the spectacle, I reason that our morning deeds are about to suffer complete disclosure. The firemen/guards attach their hoses to a nearby house and put out the flames in short order.

And then within the hour, the Prier boys are collared as the culprits in starting the fire, as they have been caught nearby with a box of matches, and confess. Oh, jeepers!

Before long the flurry blows over with the Prier boys receiving a reprimand from the guards and told to stay away from the woods forever, or some such unenforceable punishment. My brother and I have learned a couple of life-long lessons: First, never ever play with matches, and second, don't smoke cigarettes because they can make you very sick.

# Chapter Four

*A backwoods is no place for a child dressed up in the purity of white. She turns slowly around in circles, dubiously pondering the disagreeable display surrounding her in this quarter. If she could just click her heels together, like Dorothy did, she could be back among familiar sights and sounds. She clicks her heels together.*

Because Climax is considered part of the Annunciation Church parish, around the middle of July, four Sisters of Charity charge into camp from their convent in Leadville with the intention of transforming a parcel of kids from wild, woodland creatures into decent little Catholics. We must attend a two-week session of catechism classes held in the Community Center, and we do so grudgingly. Actually, I don't mind going as much as some of the kids, because it is so utterly distinctive from anything else I do. For one thing, the nuns fascinate me as I try to comprehend them.

To begin with, they are swathed from head to toe in heavy black serge garments with a bit of white surrounding their faces, called a wimple. The top part of the garb is box-shaped and makes them look totally outlandish. The Sisters have an antiseptic aura, whistle clean, with no outdoors dirt or sweat mixed in whatsoever. When they stride around the room I can always hear rosary beads click-clacking, which is useful, because then I can quickly disarm them with an alert/attentive look. If one of them ever swoops in close to my face I have determined to use the opportunity to scrutinize her face. Sister Josephine once did, and I noticed a mole with minute gray hairs above her lip. Yuck!

We are told always to address them as "Sister" which is as curious as anything else about them, I think, because my one and only real sister's name is Becky. Two are assigned to the kids in grades five through eight, and two are assigned to those of us in grades one through four. Sister Mary Joseph and Sister Giovanni are the nuns we get. We convene at eight o'clock each morning, walk home for lunch, and go again for two more hours in the afternoon. We don't get to be with Becky or Patrick and Mary Wadsworth whose classroom is upstairs, which is disappointing to me, because I always need the proximity of my sister in an unfamiliar situation, like this one. At least until I've gotten used to things.

"'Bye. See you at lunch, Becky." I say, my voice limp with disappointment.

"Don't worry, little sister." Becky waves in her customary nonchalant manner.

Well, from the first to the tenth day, Artie, Joe Wadsworth, Jacky and Jimmy Ducharme, and I, withdraw from the bigger kids and walk down a flight of stairs into a makeshift classroom, which seems to be over-burdened with brown: brown walls, brown wood floor, brown wooden chairs, large brown table up in front, and two windows with a basement view of brown dirt and gravel.

"Let's sit here," Jimmy says, pointing out five vacant seats together. We sit down.

These two nuns do like to start precisely on time. Right off before we can even get our bearings, we have to stand to say a bunch of prayers and to sing a song to the Blessed Mother; I am partial to the singing. After all of this, Sister Mary Joseph takes attendance and as our names are called we march forward to be handed a Baltimore Catechism, and then retreat quickly to our chairs. Next, Sister Giovanni arranges us in groups according to age.

"Optimum instruction and learning must occur within a brief amount of time," Sister tells us.

Jimmy and I have to move across the aisle with some other kids our age.

Jimmy and I are not among the novice Sister School attendees downstairs, because last summer we had been given instruction to prepare us to receive our first Holy Communion, and which, in fact, we did duly receive.

What First Communion preparation was, was lots of memorizing of every kind of prayer you can think of. Plus, we had to know a zillion answers to the questions set up in the catechism. This is how I remember it happening:

"Who made you?" Sister Giovanni asks me. She isn't particularly interesting to study, maybe just a bit on the plump side, because her face looks a little like it has been squeezed into the white wimple thing.

Ha, simple! "God made me."

"Why did God make you?" she asks, her eyebrows crinkling together in the middle.

"God made me so that I would love him in this world and . . . uh, be with Him in the next." The questions get progressively more difficult and complex, of course, and I have to work very hard to make all the answers stick in my brain. And, naturally, the good Sisters are there to drill us.

Sister Mary Joseph tells us that Father Horgan, at the Annunciation Church in Leadville, where the blessed ceremony is to take place, might ask one of us a question to see if we are truly worthy to receive the two sacraments: one the Holy Communion and the other, Confession.

I am likely the most rattled kid in the group when it comes to my First Confession. I kneel with the kids at the back of the church to examine my conscience. This is okay, except maybe somewhat tiresome, as I don't have much on my mind to feel guilty about. A picture in the catechism materializes in my mind showing a person's soul represented by a milk bottle that is only half full--because her sins have slurped down the other half. I try to focus on this image to get me in the mood to aim for a full bottle of milk, which is Grace.

Eventually, we queue up and when it's my turn, I open the door of the confessional and squint determinedly into the totally black alcove, but to no avail. I shuffle to the padded kneeler, which I think is a nice touch of comfort, except that I am in there overly long, and my bare knees get stuck to the surface. Kneeling there, breathing deeply in and out, I wait for Father Horgan to slide open his panel. Smells of polished wood and some other churchy one I can't identify—incense?--distract me fleetingly. When the mahogany door skims across to reveal Father's silhouette, I gawk at him for some time through a fancy grate with swirls all over it, and then I try to peek past his head into his cubicle. All I can see is the top part of his chair, and I think *Hmm, he gets to sit down while I have to kneel.*

"Ah-hmm. You may begin," he prompts. His voice is whispery and thin, like very old paper.

Oops! First slip-up. "Bless me, Father, for I have sinned. This is my first confession, and these are my sins." I say this very quickly so I won't stammer. And then, I cannot recall a single sin I'd rehearsed beforehand--second slip-up.

My mind has gone completely blank. Blink, blink, and blink. Hands sweaty, breathing erratic, eyes swimming in my head, I squeeze my brain for all I'm worth. Father is fairly patient, although he's not about to let me out of there without a couple of confessed sins. I feel like a fly stuck to flypaper.

Eventually, he starts naming some for me. "Have you disobeyed your parents?"

I press close to the screen so that none of his words get misdirected. "Yes, I did that." I hadn't planned saying that one, but I am still drawing a blank, so . . .

He clears his throat. Silence. "Ah-hem. Have you been unkind to others?"

"Yes, I did that one, too." I hadn't planned on naming that sin either, but it is a worthy one, so since my mind is still a blank snowfield it will have to do, and anyway I just really want to get out of there.

I recite my last prayer all right and listen especially carefully to the prescribed penance, as I do not want to muddle the situation further. As I tiptoe back to my pew and kneel down, I breathe a huge sigh of relief. My milk bottle is full! Or is it? I have just granted that someone else's sins are mine. I bet I just lied to Father Horgan! Oh, jeepers!

Mom makes me a First Communion dress. White as snow and whispery as a cloud, I feel completely chaste and crisp as she does up the back buttons. My socks and sandals are brand new, too. I've never worn sandals, they're not practical for playing in dirt and rocks. The most splendid feature of all is the veil that's fastened into my hair, because the netting falls to my waist, and as I gaze into the hallway mirror my appearance makes me feel like a princess, albeit a knock-kneed and pigeon-toed one.

I float, feet not quite touching the floor, as I approach the Communion rail for my very first direct face-to-face encounter with God. My turn next. Head uplifted, mouth open, tongue stuck out and the wafer being placed on it. Alas, rather than floating back to my place in the pew, I'm doing sort of a step and halt, step and halt, which causes Elva Gonzales to bump into me from behind. The wafer is stuck fast to the roof of my mouth, and my supply of saliva, which up until this moment I've taken for granted, has deserted me, and instead seems to be seeping from my fingers, which in turn makes my new white rosary and prayer book extremely slippery. Fretfulness consumes me for the remainder of Mass, as I struggle to resist sticking a finger into my mouth to scrape off the wafer's stranglehold, and thereby send it on its journey to my soul and to the milk bottle sorely in need of replenishment.

As I spiral back into the present reality of dust motes floating in the sunshine that's streaming through the windows of the room, I glance over at Artie, hoping and praying that his own First Communion event will go more smoothly than mine did.

We use a shortcut path that winds through houses from 10th Street down to 5th Street when we walk to and from Sister School. From there we stay on the gravel road which becomes White Avenue and winds through lower camp, where many houses of the White Level era were built; however, these look nice, the difference being that these houses are occupied by long-time residents and pride seeps from the stucco they are made of.

But before we draw near this neighborhood, we have to pass under the train track trestle on our way to the Community Center. A substantial four-foot by four-foot black-and-white sign at the trestle entrance warns cars to stop if a train is passing overhead. And, of course, walkers must halt, too.

This edict must *always* be heeded. One time Dad spent a long time explaining about the trestle, and I paid attention. He said that only trains going into the mine to pick up ore, or leaving with a load, use this elevated loop, no other kinds of trains travel it. And trains have come off the tracks on more than one occasion--five times have been recorded--and, in fact, one muck train had ore cars that actually went sliding down the embankment. Dad said that extreme day and nighttime changes in temperature cause the tracks to expand and contract, so that they sometimes pull apart, or at times get twisted out of alignment, which causes a train to wreck. Trains are an integral part of the mining operation and have been used at Climax since the first tunnel, called the Leal Tunnel, was bored into the mountain.

Because of this likelihood of peril, none of us ever go under the trestle before first stopping to check in both directions for an oncoming ore train--not even in the face of a double dare.

"Hey, you guys, I hear a train coming," Jimmy says one morning. "I dare you to run under right now!"

"No!" we screech above the noise of the oncoming muck train.

"I double dare you!" he challenges, his head jutting forward.

"Huh-uh!" There are no takers. And before we can counter it he runs under just as the train engine clanks across the trestle. He makes it safely to the other side, of course, but we remain motionless and stunned by his brashness for several moments.

"Whoa! Are you dumb!" Becky exclaims; and the rest of us totally concur with her.

"No, I'm not. I'm Superman! And you're chicken!" he bellows, and takes off running.

After the rest of the muck cars clatter overhead and the train continues down the tracks, we dart under the trestle and run to catch up with Jimmy.

"Ha, ha, ha!" He is laughing and jumping around like a maniac, but we just ignore him, although my face is still coated with a sweaty sheen from the fear he caused me. As we walk by the Henderson mansion, Jimmy leaps onto the low stone wall that surrounds the residence, and balances along the top, trying to peek inside.

The 1956 Resident Superintendent of Climax, Bob Henderson, resides in this mansion, which had been built in 1935. It is by far the grandest dwelling in camp, and each time I pass by, I long to see what it looks like on the inside, but I never get the chance, because the kids, Joe Pete and his sister, are several years older, and, of course, only their friends are given invitations to parties and get-togethers.

Well, now we have to sail like the wind the rest of the way down the road to the Community Church, or the nuns will commence Sister School before we arrive, and there's no telling how they might react to tardiness. Perish the thought.

Which reminds me, Father Block and Father Ryan are coming to our house for supper today. They are from Annunciation Church in Leadville and come to the Climax Community Church to say Sunday

Mass once a month, because we are after all part of the parish, sort of like their country cousins, I guess. Both priests are around my parents' age, and they are giving Dad Catholic instruction. Becky, Artie, and I have been praying for his conversion every single night since we first learned to say prayers as toddlers.

"Dear God, please bless Mommy and Daddy, Becky and Artie, my grandparents, and all my aunts, uncles, and cousins. And, please, make Daddy a Catholic. Amen."

Fathers Ryan and Block enjoy my dad's company hugely, and he likes them in turn. Dad has a lively wit that's legend in the mine. He teases the priests during suppertime and tells church jokes that make them chuckle. I don't usually get the jokes, but I enjoy the camaraderie and the jovial ambiance their visits bring into our house. After supper the grownups convene in the living room, and we are sent to bed, but we can hear laughing and talking as we succumb to sleep.

Father Block plays with us from time to time, and he smiles and laughs when we ramble on about our escapades. And he gives us a blessing each time he comes to our house.

"Father Block, come on and we'll show you our boulder field," Becky suggests one time when he is waiting for Dad to get home from the mine.

So off we go, hiking and prattling on about this and that. Then arriving at the boulders, we scramble to the top of the pile, and up he climbs, black suit, shiny shoes and all.

"May our Father in heaven bless this place with its mountain, and all the majesty that surrounds us. And, bless these three children who play here. In the name of the Father, and of the Son, and of the Holy Ghost. Amen," Father prays.

Well, Father Block and his blessings make us believe more than ever that we reside in God's country!

# Chapter Five

*The ants are furiously industrious as they go about their never-ending construction projects. The little girl lying on the ground with her chin resting on her hands watches them with keen fascination for a very long time. Suddenly, from out of nowhere a shadow falls over the scene and a booted foot unwittingly smashes a corner of the operation. The child rises up on straightened arms, and sighs.*

Toward the end of August, we hear stirrings that the Company is planning to execute a huge underground dynamite blast. Sometimes we hear small explosions coming from Phillipson Level, which is a long tunnel that bores deep into the bowels of Mount Bartlett; what we're hearing are the shots fired routinely to loosen the ore body.

--Climax Molybdenum Company had been mining under Mount Bartlett since 1917. Block cave mining created a crater during the 1930s, and the cavity grew through the years. Miners called it the Glory Hole. (All those times when we were visiting Phillipson's grave or playing on the hogback, we never considered just how perilously near the edge of the Glory Hole we were, nor did our mother.)—

The *Moly Mountain News* says that visitors, or people who drive by on Highway 91, think of the giant hole in the middle of the yellowish-brown mountain as an eyesore. Well, to Climax kids, the Glory Hole defines us and gives us our identity as much as our own names, hair, eye color, and families, and since the Glory Hole is a key feature of our surroundings; anyone who says ugly things about it is an ignorant nincompoop.

It is a honey-coated, sunshiny morning just after breakfast and my brother, sister and I are sitting on the bank in back of our house, waiting. Sluggishness and boredom are just beginning to nibble at the edges of our near filled-up-with-summer selves. And today, summertime's dawn-to-dusk playing is lying a bit heavily on us. For one thing, we've been wearing shorts and shirts with no jackets for two weeks. As a matter of fact, we feel uncomfortably warm in the 65 degrees of daytime sun, and we're beginning to long for serious, winter-like clouds to gather at the crest of Mount Bartlett.

"What do you guys want to do?" I ask Becky and Artie, hoping for inspiration that'll give us some energy and enjoyment.

"There's nothing to do," Becky says; Artie nods his agreement.

"Let's go see if the Priers or Brothers can play," Artie suggests after awhile.

"Not those stupid Brothers . . . Remember? The dam?" Beck asks and drops the stick she's been carving into the dirt with, and then sweeps us with a stern glance.

"Oh. Yeah," Artie and I say at the same time. We agree not to make up friends with those Brothers anytime soon, and that's for sure. What happened was:

For an entire week we've been putting all of our efforts into building a dam with some of the 10th street kids over by the Ducharme's house, where a small stream trickles down from the high melting snowfields, and never seems to dry up all summer long. Everyone keeps digging and digging until we have a very nice hole beside the creek, and then we dig some more, so that some of the creek's runoff will flow directly into the hole. The result of all this hard labor puts the brag into all of us. We make boats out of tree bark and sticks, and play at sinking ships, which amuses us for a while, but not as much as the digging has done.

Anyway, before you know it, trouble starts because someone's boat- -who knows whose?--gets swamped and capsizes, followed by a friendly battle of destroying everyone's boats. After a while, though, Mikey Brothers gets a snoot full of mud, and an all-out war results.

Eventually, every one of us is coated with muck, but by that time Mikey's older sisters, Ava Lou and Bonnie, decide to tear the dickens out of the dam by stomping part of a mud wall in with their feet. The rest of us, screaming and yelling, chase them to the border of their back yard where they have taken refuge.

"You're in for it now!" Jimmy Ducharme yells, his voice full of snap. Times like these I'm good and glad he's on my side of the mayhem.

"Yeah, you have to leave your yard sometime--and when you do . . . look out!" This from Evelyn Prier, who could be mean as hot tar sometimes, like the tar the Company men were spreading all over our roof yesterday, to keep the winter snow from wearing it down to leaks, because ours is a flattop house and a whole lot of snow piles up up there during the long wintertime.

--Taking care of the camp houses and other buildings in Climax was handled by the Surface Maintenance Department; all the residents had to do was call, tell the department what needed to be done and the problem would be dealt with within twenty-four hours. A family could have the entire interior--and outside trim, too--of their house painted every single summer, merely because they fancied a change. If any household had plumbing or electrical problems, this crew would see to the trouble promptly, and in a friendly manner, and at no cost to the employees. Employees were charged a very modest house rent, but upkeep was a responsibility the Company took upon itself. In 1956, the monthly rental rate (per room) for a house like ours on 10th Street was $14.75. The Company absorbed the cost of taxes, insurance, and depreciation.

Surface Maintenance didn't bother with yard work, though, since the summers were so short it wasn't worth the sweat and toil to plant grass, bushes, or any other type of landscaping.--

Everyone's yards look all the same--dirt and rocks; the few exceptions include Mr. Montaine down on 7th Street. He has grass, but he spends all his hours off work outside, babying his patch of green. We always see him when we walk by, all bent over his yellow-and-orange Iceland poppies, or watering his grass with a garden hose. He has his green-and-yellow-and-orange all fenced in, too, so that none of us "young hooligans," as he calls us, can trample on his pride and joy. To tell you the truth, I wouldn't mind for a minute if we had some green grass growing in our yard. This is maybe the only minus I can think of, when it comes to living in Climax.

Anyway, sitting on that bank with heads resting on hands is no good for our summertime amusement.

"I'm going inside," Becky tells us, with a voice heavy with sighs.

Artie starts to dig a mine tunnel beside his leg. It seems like we're always doing this to pass the time, digging. After a while, he says he needs a spoon to dig with, since the sharp rock he has isn't up to the job.

"I'll go in an get two spoons for us," I offer, with nothing better to do, and I'm off to the silverware drawer, hoping Mom's busy someplace besides the kitchen.

I'm back quick as a wink, and we set to work. Artie likes to blast his holes with lots of loud explosive sounds that he's good at. I make blasting noises too, but not as well. We've gathered some toy trucks and 'dozers to help our play along, so now we start flattening out a road to drive them on. Just at this time Danny and David Prier come bolting out their back door, and up the incline to us.

"Hey, you guys! Did you hear there's going to be a big blast in the Glory Hole?" Danny asks at the top of his lungs.

"And it's going to be tomorrow!" David adds, excitement making his face all red in spots.

Well, no. As a matter of fact, Artie and I haven't heard a single word about this blast.

"Humph. Who says?" I ask, with a voice thick with scorn at the lies the two of them have no trouble telling, just for the fun of it.

"Everybody knows. It talks about it in yesterday's *Moly Mountain News*," Danny says, whose keyed-up talking causes the gum in his mouth to fall out.

--The *Moly Mountain News* was a twice-weekly bulletin that kept the camp residents up to date on news and weather, along with a calendar of upcoming events, and anything else that might be of interest to the community. The bulletin was published faithfully by the Public Relations Department that was housed in the guardhouse. Later on, a smaller version, more of a flier, called the *Hi Grade*, was distributed to employees and their families.—

The four of us turn our heads to gaze up at the Glory Hole on Mt. Bartlett. Even with all our imaginations working together, like the insides of a machine, we cannot picture what this big blast will look like, or what changes it might bring into our lives.

--It was back in the mine's early days that miners began blasting with sticks of dynamite to loosen up the ore in a tunnel; this method was called "shrinkage stope mining." Two miners, working in tandem, would drill a hole and the other would shove in a stick of dynamite. Everyone would be cleared from the area, the entryways guarded so that no one would happen into the line of fire, and then the two would run about fifty yards away, light a fuse, yell out, "Fire in the hole!" and hunker down for the blast. This was done all the time; back then it was an everyday occurrence, in fact.

As the mine developed, and conditions changed, it became evident that the owners needed to transition to "block cave mining" to cut high production costs. So in May, 1933, more than a hundred thousand pounds of dynamite exploded deep in the bowels of Mt. Bartlett, shattering several hundred thousand tons of ore, and creating a new era in underground mining history. But once again, in the summer of 1956, a big blast was necessary to dislodge an unyielding bridge of rock above the Phillipson Level. Other big blasts would follow in the course of the mine's life--one of titanic magnitude in May of '64, the Coyote Blast, loosened one and a half million tons of ore. However, it is this particular blast in 1956 that sent shivers up and down the spines of the 10th Street kids, and everybody else who, at the time, called Climax home.--

That evening during supper all we can talk about is tomorrow's Big Blast, and the bonus amount of excitement it will offer us. Even having a circus come to camp couldn't surpass this event--not that a circus ever would.

"Dad, what's it going be like?" I ask in wide-eyed wonderment, attempting to swallow three lima beans without chewing.

"Well, your mother will take you people on down across the highway by the store. You'll watch from over there," he explains simply. This is what he calls his children, "you people."

"How's come we can't stay right here and watch?" Artie wants to know. He likes to make animals out of mashed potatoes at the table, and he's just made a . . . something.

"Don't play with your food, boy." And then Dad continues in a calm, steady voice, "All kinds of rock will be blasted from the mountain, and no one knows for sure which way it'll fall."

"You mean big rocks and boulders could fall on our house, and squash it flat?" Becky asks, maybe thinking about our nearby boulder field, which I am certainly now thinking carefully about.

Dad answers her in an utterly soulful tone, "Could. Just better wait and see what happens." As he says this last bit, he looks right down the table at Mom. She has been sort of quiet throughout this entire mealtime talk, which gets me wondering about stuff even harder.

The next day starts out lemony-bright with a snap to it. Mom hustles us through our breakfast, and then buzzes around outside hanging sheets out to dry, then she takes the sheets back off the clotheslines and throws them into the dryer, which makes me ask, "Mom, how come you took the sheets down before they could get dry in the sweet mountain air?" That's what she always says, "There's nothing like the sweet mountain air for drying clothes."

"Well, DoGo, I had second thoughts, because the blasting will no doubt leave thick, yellow dust in the air. No need to get that all over my sheets, huh?"

Both of my parents are very big on nicknames. As the story goes, one time when I was a very little kid, we visited the Wadsworths, and their large, longhaired dog "DoGo," was sleeping on the sofa. The tale goes on that I petted and hugged the old, flea-bitten dog the whole time we were visiting, and then I cried inconsolably when it was time to leave. So they bestowed upon me this horrid nickname that I just hate almost to the point of making tears come to my eyes. If they slip up and call me this in front of company, I really do cry tears of embarrassment. I have a few more nicknames, but I won't mention them unless I have to, which I do not.

We have a yellow-and-white '55 Olds that Dad drives to work over at Stork Level. He's been on straight days for a while now, and this is nice, because when he's on swing or graveyard shifts we hardly ever get to see him. He always takes a lunch packed in a black lunch bucket that the miners call a "pie can." Dad wears regular clothes to work, but when he gets to the mine "dry"--a changing room--he changes into his "diggers":

overalls, flannel shirt, warm jacket, steel-toed boots and a hard hat. Plus, he always wears safety glasses underground. Dad says that the one item that he can never overlook is the brass tag that identifies him, because if a brass tag isn't turned in at the end of a shift, it indicates that the owner is still in the mine and could be hurt, or worse.

My dad is a stickler for safety because he says safety is a miner's best ally, and, he adds emphatically, Climax is a very safe mine. The company gives out safety awards once a year. One time we got a set of carving knives made with moly steel. Last night, Dad said that all the miners would ride out of the mine in "man trips," special train cars for miners to ride in, and that they would watch the big blast from a safe distance.

Right about now, Arlene Prier pulls their station wagon into our driveway, because our car is down at Stork Level, and anyway, Mom is just learning how to drive. We pile in and ride with the Priers down to the Fremont Trading Post, where we find a fairly satisfactory parking place to watch Mt. Bartlett's immense spectacle. So many people have already gathered that I can't even begin to count them. "Hundreds probably," I think aloud.

"Mom, can we get out, please?" Becky asks for all our sakes, because we cannot bear being cooped up in a car.

"Yes, fine, but stay close by," she tells us, and goes back to chatting with Mrs. Prier.

We spy a site on a bit of an incline, and dodge people to get to it. From this great vantage point we're sure that we won't miss a lick of the action.

After we've settled down to wait, Evelyn and Becky decide to go back to the car and ask our moms if they can go into the store to buy candy for all of us.

"Good idea, but you better hurry up, or you'll miss the show," Danny warns.

Well, now we've been waiting almost an hour and nothing has happened whatsoever. Becky and Evelyn return with a bag of black licorice whips for us to share.

"This is dumb," David whines after we've been sitting and watching the mountain for a long time. I look at him and notice a sticky black ring around his mouth.

"Ho! Just wait and see! Something will happen pretty soon," I say hopefully, crossing my fingers. "Anyway, your face looks ridiculous--"

*KaaBoom!* It sounds like a gigantic bomb exploding . . . whatever that might sound like. And then the siren—the mine whistle--starts in and continues to squall unceasingly for the next hour or so. The ground trembles and quakes under our feet. A huge cloud of dust and smoke rises straight into the air and covers almost the whole entire mountain. In fact, we cannot even see the mountain at all. Well, that was the Big Blast!

We have to stay around here for most of the rest of the day, until the dust and smoke settle, and the Company says its safe to return to our homes. So we get to have a whopping treat and eat lunch in the luncheonette at the Fremont Trading Post. This is Climax's very own community shopping center with everything anyone could want to buy, and pretty much every employee does spend his entire paycheck here-- "payroll deduction," my dad calls it. Inside there is a grocery store, clothing shop, appliance place, beauty parlor, barbershop, and a beer joint called the Slop Chute." My parents are not ones to go in there, because they say it's a place of drunken behavior and carrying on.

--My dad recently told me that he knew of plenty of instances wherein men on his various crews throughout the years would stack up a debt of $500 or more, in maybe a four-month period of time. The Fremont Trading Post would then take every penny of the miner's bi-monthly paycheck, except for $20. Truly desperate, the man would pack up his family and what belongings he could fit into his car, and leave camp under cover of darkness.

I never got a chance to see inside the beer joint until I landed a summer job at the luncheonette during my college years. So it wasn't until then that I discovered it was not at all the forbidding place I'd imagined in my early years, just some booths, a smallish bar, and a jukebox, with the semi-darkness lighted by lamps during the day, because it happened to be windowless.—

At last, we obtain the "all clear" from the guards and drive back up to our houses, kids heads straining out of the car windows to see if any rocks or boulders had been catapulted into camp during the Big Blast. Nope. But, the good old Glory Hole is more gigantic than it was this morning. All in all, it turned out to be quite an exhilarating adventure for us, and after that day we spend heaps of time playing miners blowing up the hill behind our house with make-believe dynamite, Artie's truck and steam shovels, and Mom's spoons and stuff. We eventually construct a town complete with streets, buildings and houses, transforming that ordinary orange dirt bank into a miniature replica of Climax.

# Chapter Six

*It's no wonder that you're chilled and dripping wet if you insist on playing outside in the rain, little girl. Why don't you take some good advice and stay indoors for a change? But, the house is stuffy warm and the child knows that the walls and floors will offer no surprises--no laughter, nor tears either, for that matter, so she runs out the door and back into the wet chill.*

Occasionally people come all the way up to Climax to visit. Both sets of my grandparents have visited us, as well as aunts and uncles and cousins, at one time or another. Last summer my grandparents came from Ohio, and we went to Denver to meet them at Union Station where the trains arrive and depart; we drove home over Battle Mountain and Tennessee Pass, a very steep part of Highway 24 approaching Climax from the Leadville side.

This is what happened on the way home: Dad decides to stop the car on the side of the road so that we can show Grandma and Grandpa Vincent what it looks like over the edge, how it plummets to a river way down in the ravine. Everyone climbs out of the car, Becky, Artie and I tumbling over one another like puppies. We clamor around a bridge called "Lover's Leap," peering over the edge. But my poor grandpa's so scared that he almost faints, and he is ghostly pale and wobbly. My dad helps him shuffle back to the car, and says he's really sorry that Grandpa feels sick from looking down. This bowls me over, because I guess I'm just so used to looking down at deep gorges and looking up at high peaks, that for someone to be fazed by any of it comes as a shocker.

My grandpa never does get to feeling well during this trip; in fact, he is stricken with pneumonia, and has to stay in Climax Hospital for two weeks, where the doctors and nurses take very good care of him, but they don't make him completely well.

Aside from the drive home and Grandpa being sick, nothing notable happens during their visit, except that my grandma thinks Artie is the funniest character on the face of the earth, funnier even than Red Skelton and Jack Benny, combined. All it takes is for Artie to make one

47

of his goofy faces, or cavort around the room, and she collapses in gales of laughter, wiping tears from her eyes. For Pete's sake, I cannot see what it is that Grandma finds so hilarious about my brother.

Eventually, Grandpa's condition worsens because of his age, and of course the high altitude, so Grandma has to take him back to Columbus on the train, and Dad decides to go along to help out--not a relaxing vacation that time for anyone, I guess.

Meanwhile, a week or so after the Big Blast, Mom says at breakfast, "Your Uncle Dick and Aunt Jean are coming from Ohio for a visit."

"Yippee! Are Ricky and Valerie coming, too?" I ask, while trying to sneak an extra spoonful of sugar onto my cornflakes.

"You are a complete idiot sometimes, Debbie. What do you think? That people just leave their kids to fend for themselves while the parents go on vacation?" Becky says sourly, as she finishes her cereal.

"Well, everybody knows I'm not a complete idiot. I get straight A's, don't I?" I am always shattered by my sister's occasional criticisms.

Mom ignores this interchange, and thinks aloud, "We'll put you three girls together, and Ricky can sleep in Artie's room with him." She finishes wiping down the countertops, folds the dishtowel, and then, leaving the room, she turns and says, "Girls, get the clothes hung out on the lines before you run off to play."

"Boy. Why doesn't Artie, the baby, ever have chores to do?" Becky whines, as she carries the clothesbasket outside.

"He's still over at Jacky Ducharme's where he spent the night. He's always getting to do fun stuff that you and me don't get to do, just because we're girls," I commiserate, as I hand the end of a sheet to her.

Becky and I walk over to the swings, looking for something to do after we finish hanging out the clothes. School doesn't start for three and a half more weeks, and it's becoming more and more of a challenge to find ways to amuse ourselves.

"Well, I hope Ricky doesn't think he's such a smart aleck, like he did last summer when we were back at their house. He's nothing but a big old boaster, huh, Debbie?"

I nod my agreement. More often than not, I totally agree with my sister, because she's typically right about things. In fact, just the other evening we were playing kick-the-can up the street in front of the Wadsworth's, and...

As the sun sinks behind Chalk Ridge, the mountains and sky are bathed in pinks and lavenders. Quite a few kids are out playing during these hours after supper, although daylight is rapidly fading into darkness. It's actually a wonderment that *we* are still outdoors; Mom has not called us home yet.

All the kids are getting along well and having a lot of fun playing "Annie, Annie Over." Then Patrick and Jimmy leave, but they come back with a metal pail, the kind Mom uses for scrubbing floors. Presently, the two boys fill the bucket to the brim with gravel rocks from the roadside, and start firing rocks up at the streetlight, and all of us have to scatter, crouching as the rocks rain back down to the street.

"How's come you guys are doing that?" Artie asks, who's watching open-mouthed with Joe and Jacky.

"Can't you see those flying things up around the light?" Patrick asks the group. "Well, those are bats! We're trying to ding them to see if they'll fly down lower, and then we can get a holda one." He throws a whole handful of rocks into the sky, laughing like a hyena. Jimmy follows suit.

"You guys better stop doing that!" my sister warns them in a grave tone of voice.

"Yeah, if the paddy wagon comes along and the guards see what you're doing, they'll write your names down in the black book for sure," I add to her dire warning, while keeping my voice from breaking into a tremor.

"Oh, Becky and Debbie Vincent, the two biggest scaredy cats in camp. Why don't you go home and suck on a baby bottle?" Jimmy sneers, sounding like his most cruel and insufferable self.

"We're pretty gosh darn sick of you and your flapping tongue, so there!" Becky declares, stomping right up close to him, glowering.

Well, he hauls off and slugs Beck on the arm, and then they tussle around right there in the street. Patrick, Mary, and Catherine Wadsworth and the Priers and everyone think it's a darn circus, and they all start cheering and making a ruckus. But the younger ones, including me, stand around slack-jawed, watching. In short order, I get a jumpy stomach and tears flood down my face. And before I can stop myself, I'm blubbering and screeching at Jimmy that he'd better get up off my sister and just leave us alone.

Patrick takes hold of his friend's arm and says, "Ah, just leave her alone, Jimmy. Her sister's making too much noise!"

So he lets my sister get up, and then everyone just heads for home. But before we go into our house Becky says, "Just wait until Ricky gets here tomorrow. I'll sic him on that dim-witted blockhead, Jimmy, and then we'll see who's the clever one." She's not hurt, just shaken, and thoroughly incensed.

Well, I've never thought of my cousin, Ricky, as being much of a toughie, but who knows what can happen? Becky frequently does have a good idea or two about how things will be.

Our relatives get to Climax mid-morning the following day, and we get a telephone call from the guardhouse.

--Ever since WWII, when the federal government was worried that someone might try to sabotage the Climax Molybdenum Company because moly was so important to the war effort, there has been a guardhouse and a gate into camp, and a chain-link fence surrounding the whole place.

Every employee at the time he is hired must be fingerprinted by the Protection Department and issued a badge with a picture ID with his number on it. Whenever we drive into camp from anyplace, Dad has to show his badge to the guards. Every employee must wear his badge all the time while on Company property. And anyone who comes to Climax for a visit has to stop at the guardhouse and wait until an acquaintance comes down to escort them to a house, or one of the ten apartment buildings. If a visitor is there on business, a temporary pass is issued.—

Dad drives down to meet our relatives and they follow him up to our house. My folks have planned a picnic lunch at Officers' Gulch on Ten Mile Creek down by Frisco, just about ten miles from Climax, which is where the creek's name comes from, I guess. Art and Becky and I are very excited about picnicking.

Mom has been in the kitchen all morning, making potato salad and baking a chocolate cake. These are two of my favorite foods that she makes, after I pick the onions out of my salad, that is. When we first moved to Climax she says she had a dickens of a time baking a cake; it would always fall flat as a pancake, or she'd get a big hole right in the center after she took it out of the oven while it was cooling. Mom's not one to give up, though, so, after many attempts and failures, she came across a high-altitude cookbook. Now her cakes are the best anywhere.

It is when we are showing off the boulder field to Valerie and Ricky that we hear Mom calling us. Funny, we always hear her even from a long way off—it must be some kind of a high-country phenomenon. We walk, instead of run, with our cousins, because they're both real tired already, and we haven't even been doing anything, like climbing up to the tanks, or playing in the broken-down trees. Sheesh! I don't think Ricky'll be much of a threat to Jimmy.

The drive down Fremont Pass takes us past the tailing pond at Robinson Flats. Tailing is the stuff left over from processing the moly ore; it's grayish-white, like a begrimed snowfield in the summertime. Our relatives stare at the view as if it were the most dreadful blot on the landscape. Dad explains how water-cycling works in the mining operation, and how careful the Company tries to be with the environment, which makes them feel better, I guess, because there is no more complaining from them about the unsightliness of the tailing pond.

--Today there is a historical marker near Climax on Highway 91, detailing three small mining camps, Kokomo, Robinson, & Recen, that existed on this site in the late 1800s. The Ten Mile Mining District boasted twelve hotels, twenty saloons, four sawmills, five general stores, two shoemakers, five bakeries, a post office, a newspaper and several brothels. Eventually, fires destroyed the camps and only a few buildings were still standing during the Climax years, which allowed for a convenient place for the tailing to be collected.--

Forests of pine, spruce, conifer, and aspen follow us down the canyon highway. When we get to within a few miles of the campground, gray, granite chalk cliffs rise to the blue sky on both sides of the highway.

We turn into the Officers' Gulch Campground, and my dad parks the car within easy walking distance of the creek. A campfire is built straight away, and all the picnic supplies are set atop a brown wooden table. We long to be off exploring, but hunger keeps us hanging around the campfire. Hotdogs, burgers, potato salad, and cake fill us up, and the fire warms us--the campground is deep in shadow most of the time, because of the high cliffs all around.

After lunch, my dad and uncle go for a hike into the trees, and we sit around poking sticks into the fire, which is very satisfying, considering the way Mom and Dad feel about us playing with fire at any other time. Presently, the two men are making fast tracks back to us.

"Dick and I were just now face-to-face with a goddamned mountain lion!" Dad says, with a husky breathlessness.

*Jeepers! He must be really upset and terrified cussing in front of us like that!* I think. My poor uncle is pacing around, and looking back up at that hill with something close to pure panic plastering his face.

"Where, Dad? Where is the mountain lion?" Artie asks with glee and exhilaration, dancing from one foot to the other.

"Up beyond that rock outcropping, see? There by that small stand of aspens? There she goes! Must have just finished with a rabbit lunch, or she might have paid us more attention!" he exclaims, still breathing rapidly.

"Let's go up and try to follow her!" Artie suggests to us. We've been stretching our necks and squinting mightily at the area in the forest where Dad was pointing.

"No! You people stay around here; no need to go off borrowing trouble from a wildcat," Dad commands firmly, looking squarely into our eyes.

"Hey, Val and Ricky, I remember one other time when we were picnicking, just down below the Robinson Dam, and Dad spotted a mountain lion. There was a sheepherder's hut somewhere nearby, and the sheep were summer grazing. Dad saw the wildcat clenching a lamb in her jaws, and quickly shooed us into the car." And, because I have their full attention, I continue the yarn at full throttle. "Anyway, he stopped by the guardhouse when we got back to camp, and reported the sighting; and the guards went over to the place and shot the mountain lion, because they said that she might have come into camp, which would pose a great danger to people, particularly small children!"

Well, this story really impresses my cousins, and my face shows the satisfaction that my heart feels at having achieved such a successful performance.

--During those particular years, there were two ranchers who brought their sheep to the high meadows around the Robinson Dam for summer grazing. As a matter of interest, one man was Bob Burford, who later was named Chief of the Bureau of Land Management by President Reagan.--

Us Vincent kids are still feeling slightly glum because we're not permitted to track and observe the wildcat, so we walk dejectedly across dark brown dirt and pine needles to the creek, and our cousins follow along ambivalently. Before long, we happen upon a couple of large creek rocks to park ourselves atop.

"Hey, let's go wading, you guys!" Becky shouts, in order to be heard over the vast noise that the creek makes, as it bounces and leaps over rocks. She thinks for a minute, and then sighs, "Guess we better ask for permission first."

"We'll go," I say, taking my cousin by the hand. "Come on, Val. Come with me." She is between Artie and me in age, and Ricky is a year older than Becky. Val and I are fast friends during this visit.

Mom and Aunt Jean walk back to the creek with us to look the situation over. We find Beck, Art, and Ricky throwing rocks into the water like they're part of an Olympic competition, or something.

Mom says, with furrowed brow, "The river's running much too swiftly; you kids'll get carried away if you get in that water."

"Ah! Please, Mom, please?" we say, pleading, which from time to time works with her.

"No. And that's final." Mom and Aunt Jean amble off, taking our good times and laughter away with them.

Oh, well. For the next hour or so, we throw rocks into the swift waters. Before long, we're dropping in rocks that are big enough to make sizable splashes. By this time our jackets and pants are thoroughly soaked, and freezing cold.

"Bet you can't jump to that big rock out there without falling in!" Artie challenges.

Becky is dare-devil enough to take on the challenge. She leaps, and lands on her feet, and then over-balances, waving both arms in the air for a split second, before she shrieks shrilly and plunges in. Foamy white freezing water shocks her, momentarily sucking the breath out of her.

"We'll get you out!" I holler, as I splash and stagger into the icy waters to help her. Artie jumps in right after, and grabs for a rock to hold to, but his reach falls short and . . . down he goes! All three of us flail and thrash around in the stream, trying to get footing, but the water rushes by so swiftly that we keep getting knocked off balance.

Making our slow way to the bank, Becky says, at the top of her lungs, "Well, we might as well go wading, now. We're already in trouble anyway."

Artie and I have to agree with her reasoning, because it makes perfect sense to us.

"Come on, you guys! It's fun!" Artie says to our Ohio cousins.

"Not me! It's too cold," Ricky yells, over the noise of the creek. Valerie just keeps shaking her head, no, no, no.

We three frolic in the water for a good while--until our feet and legs are a deep shade of purple, and pretty much numb to any feeling.

Sloshing and dripping, we head back to the campfire.

"We fell in!" I say to the adults playing pinochle at the picnic table.

"Becky fell off a rock first, and then me and Debbie had to rescue her before the icy water carried her off!" Artie tries explaining to anyone who'll listen to such a lame excuse.

Mom and Dad don't look too happy seeing us with chattering teeth and soaked clothes, but they use the tablecloth to wrap me up in, after I peel out of my freezing wet stuff, and bundle me into the car. Becky and Artie get warmed in old blankets from the car trunk, and are hustled into the car for our ride back to Climax.

Back in camp, the azure skies have turned leaden, and a rumbling commences from over by the Sleeping Indian--a local name for Mt. Arkansas that describes its shape: three humps of ridges, feet, folded arms, head with a sharp, jutting nose and crowned by a realistic-looking headdress fanning out. And just now, the Sleeping Indian's drumbeat announces that we're in for a thunderstorm.

The following day dawns bright and shiny clear, although soggy from last night's rain. Yesterday we had promised Ricky and Val a piece of fool's gold to take back with them, but we had to wait until this morning to go out looking for some. So now we head over to the boulder field armed with Dad's hammer and a tire iron, that have to be sneaked out of the garage, because he says he's fed up with his tools missing when he needs to use them. We're off to the boulders to "find gold," we keep repeating to our cousins. Of course, we know about several rocks that have lots of iron pyrite and mica showing on the surface. The trick is to find a deposit that's effortless to extract.

Artie, Becky and I take turns whacking and crushing an assortment of rocks. When it's my turn to use the hammer, I manage to bash the living daylights out of two fingers.

"Ouch! Owie, owie, owie! I smashed my fingers!" I wail at the top of my lungs.

"Let me see!" Becky says. Everyone peers at my hand for a minute. "You're going to lose both fingernails. They'll fall right off after a while, just wait and see," my sister tells me, shaking her head with concern and regret.

Well, now, this prediction generates gales of tears and carrying on, because the suggestion of my fingernails falling off deeply disturbs me.

"Better stop blubbering, or Dad might come up here, and then he'll see his tools, and then we'll be in big trouble," Artie says, and he pats my knee sympathetically.

The thought impresses me enough for my tears to ebb into sniffles and hiccups. I have to wipe my eyes and nose on my shirtsleeve, because, naturally, no one has a tissue in their pocket.

In the meantime, Becky has been explaining to Ricky with sage exaggeration about a mean bully who badly needs to be taught a lesson. Our cousin shows only mild interest, as Beck steams herself up to an indignant plateau. She embellishes each story with brutal details, ending with an account of her humiliating pummeling the night before their arrival.

"So why are you telling me all these lame stories?" he asks, his attention being absorbed by the nearly completed removal of the fool's gold sample.

She stands, brushes her hands off on her jeans, and speaks with scathing sarcasm, "If you won't beat him up for me, then you must be related to him, and not us. Because it's obvious that you are just as dense and cowardly as Jimmy Ducharme is." She turns on her heel and stomps away with admirable aplomb.

Eventually, we manage to extract a good-sized, very shiny chunk of genuine fool's gold; but my smashed fingers, and Becky's lingering black cloud, leaves me with dampened enthusiasm. Ricky and Val depart for home with a coveted Climax souvenir, but with my sister's honor undefended.

# Chapter Seven

*Little girls are made of sugar and spice and everything nice; little boys are made of*
*snips and snails and puppy dog tails. The child dressed in long denim pants and*
*a plaid flannel shirt with her hair folded up under a ball cap longs to be made of*
*snips, snails, and puppy dog tails. Besides, sugar and spice are boring, and nice*
*doesn't really mean anything, at all.*

At long last the Labor Day weekend is upon us, and then it's only one
more week until school starts. All we can talk about is the forthcoming
school year; we anticipate school days as much as we do everything else
in Climax.

"Who do you think I'll get for my teacher this year, Becky?" I ask, as
we swing slowly back and forth at the playground.

"Hmmm. Might be Mrs. Ross or maybe Mrs. Yanish. Remember, I
had Mrs. Ross; she's real nice," she answers, dragging a stick in the dirt
hypnotically keeping rhythm with the swing.

"I hope I get Mrs. Ross. I need a stick," I murmur, eyeing hers.

"Here. You can have this one, if you want. I'm going in and get ready
to go to Leadville." And off she goes, leaving me with my musings.

I linger at the swings, dragging the stick for a few more minutes
before I heave a sigh and follow my sister. "Hey, wait up for me!" I call
out, but she's too far ahead and maybe doesn't hear me. And then, what
do you know? Here come Jacky and Jimmy Ducharme loaded down with
camping gear. Artie's with them, and they're heading for our backyard
tent.

"What you guys doing with all that stuff, anyway?" I ask the boys.

Artie and Jacky are both wearing Davy Crocket coonskin hats. I kind
of wish I had one, but only mildly.

"We're camping out tonight in the tent, that's what," Jimmy says,
which is more attention than he usually directs my way.

"So, did Mom say you can? Because we're going down to Leadville
after lunch, you know."

"Yeah, I know. Don't worry. We're camping out tonight after we get back," Artie says, dragging the bottom end of a sleeping bag that's come lose from its ties.

"Oh. Darn! I wish I could camp out with you guys," I say wistfully to no one in particular.

"Ho! That'll be the day! You're just a dumb girl," Jimmy scoffs.

"Oh, yeah? Well, I hope that one of these days someone just flattens you out on the biggest dirt pile imaginable and leaves you for the vultures to clean up."

"Oh, yeah? Who's going to do that?" He laughs, his words sting and I beat a hasty retreat.

Dejected and inflamed, I dart into the house letting the back screen door slam behind me. "Mom! Where are you?" I call out from the kitchen.

"Come into the bathroom so that I can braid your hair, DoGo." Mom says from the hallway.

I sit on the toilet seat while she works on my hair.

"Mom, can I camp out in the tent tonight with Artie and his friends?" I beg, my voice burdened with arduous longing.

"We've been all through this time and again, Debbie. You know that I will not change my mind."

"But, why?" I demand with a tear-soaked voice. "Why can't I, Mom?"

"Because you're a girl," she says simply, as she leaves the bathroom.

"I wish I was a boy," I say vehemently to the retreating back of her dress. And I sit there moping and contemplating a world suddenly altered that would allow me the freedom bestowed upon boys practically from their cradles.

--Two brief decades later, after bashing through the barricades and storming the walls of the establishment, the battle to bring about equal rights for women was won. Had I known that this time was, relatively speaking, right around the corner, I would have entreated the "movers and shakers" of the '70s to start burning their bras during the summer evening of 1956. Actually, my parents were very supportive of Becky and me when it came to our education and aspirations to fulfill any occupational dreams we might harbor. Of course, we later came to realize that all the fuss during our youth was most likely about keeping our sanctity safe, rather than about conspiring to allot us lowly second-class status.—

"Better get changed. We're leaving for Leadville as soon as Dad gets home," Becky reports, as I drag morosely into our bedroom. So, I change into my blue peddle-pushers and matching top.

The yellow Olds is spotlessly polished because Mom washed it with the hose this morning. We three clamber into the backseat and jockey for the window seats. I'm relegated to the middle position, and because my mood has dampened my spirits considerably, a window ranking offers no consolation, so why fight for one?

Out on Highway 91 we are just going around the hairpin curve at Stork Level, only five minutes from the gatehouse, when a scuffle breaks out among us kids.

"Mom! Becky just called me a bad name!" Artie whines.

"I did not. I just said that his coonskin cap looks pretty darned dumb," she offers as a sensible explanation, her face the picture of virtuous innocence.

"Mom! Everybody is messing my hair up!" I blurt out three minutes later. Our complaints are directed to Mom since Dad's concentration is confined to the highway.

Next Artie snivels. "Ouch! Stop sitting right on top of me and scoot over on your on side. I'm telling on you." And he bawls out, "Mom! The girls won't scoot over and give me some room!" The hands attempting to shush him muffle his voice.

"Okay. That's enough. You people stand with your hands on the back of the seat," Dad says sternly. "And the next time I have to tell you, I'll pull over and stop the car."

Boy, oh boy! This is not good, because now we have to try to keep our feet balanced, or we'll topple over going around a curve, and this road has more darn curves than straight, that's for sure. In no time at all we are giggling and bumping back and forth into one another, until down I go with Artie on top of me. From the floorboards I ask timidly if we can sit down on the seat again.

"Okay. But no more horseplay." Dad tells us.

--Leadville is the closest town to Climax, and in 1956, seemed distinguished and substantial to me. A hundred thousand people had lived in the town and the surrounding hills during its glory days when silver was king, although it only had a population of about four thousand by this time.

Large old buildings lined Harrison Avenue, its main street, and on the side streets, marching both to the east and to the west of it, one saw mostly Victorian-style homes and bungalows in various states of disrepair. Traveling on any of the eastside streets, one was greeted by the sight of hundreds of mine dumps dotting the hilly terrain and, until quite recently, huge piles of black slag deposits--rather smug in their ugliness--at the south end of Harrison Avenue. And then, along Highway 24 edging the southern flank of the town, lay California Gulch, a renowned site where gold and silver deposits made millionaires of a few lucky Leadville miners. This particular place remains a ghost of glory days gone by, left by thousands of miners in a state of unsightly abandonment: a rusty creek bed with ochre banks, the only reminder of long-ago prosperity.

Becky was always getting summer jobs at historical places like the Healy House and the Matchless Mine when she was in high school, and she was a walking, talking guidebook of information. She even got to work at Climax Moly Company as a tour guide in 1964. She came home from work one day very excited because she had met and interviewed Otis Archie King, a prospector during the early 1900s on Mt. Bartlett and author of *Grey Gold*. She told us that he was very old, but brilliant and spirited to listen to. I was unimpressed, as I had never heard of the person.

That was the Leadville of 1956. Today, the small city has experienced yet another renaissance, and is once again thriving, this time as a tourist town, as well as serving as a bedroom community for people working in the bordering ski resort towns--only a fraction of Leadville natives and transplanted Climax people remain as residents. —

Once in town we park on Harrison Avenue near the Safeway store; we shop here for groceries a couple times a month. Mom and Dad don't believe in owing their souls to the company store, (which is a good song that I like a lot) so they come here and spend cold, hard cash. In the store Becky, Artie and I find a place to perch next to the book and magazine racks, so that we can read comic books and promptly become absorbed in them. My favorites are "Betty and Veronica," "Donald Duck," and "Dennis the Menace." Once in a while we're permitted to buy one, but not very often.

After awhile, Mom beckons to and us says that we can pick out some Big Chief tablets and new boxes of crayons and other stuff for school, which pleases and excites us.

After the groceries are packed in the trunk, we cross the street to the Golden Burro Café. We prefer a two-in-one corner booth, so that Mom and Dad can talk to each other and also with the owner, who generally stops by our table, with minimal disturbance from us. Each time we come we order cheeseburgers and French fries, which we love, but we always have to get milk for the beverage.

"Why don't you people order the roast beef or the pork chops?" Dad asks each time, but, in the end, he allows us to select what we want because eating out at a restaurant is a family treat.

Sometimes we go shopping in other stores, like JC Penney's or Matlock's 5&10, and we get to go to the Fox Theatre down the street when a wholesome movie is showing.

On the trip home us kids leave each other pretty much alone because even playful pups get worn out.

A dusky indigo is nudging the pink horizon as we pull into our driveway, and we are out of the car and away in a flash.

"I'm going to go get Jacky and Jimmy," Artie calls out on the run.

"Me, too," I say, trailing on his heels.

A bit later, the back yard is in semidarkness because of the lights in the house, but I have to be careful not to stumble, as I scoot in and out of the back door supplying the lucky ducks in the tent with abundant treats.

"Here's some Kool Aide, you guys," I say to the closed tent flap, while balancing a heavy jug and plastic cups in my hands.

"What's the password?" Jimmy asks, his voice cloaked in secrecy.

"I don't know. You guys didn't tell me one." I hear giggling from the shadowy recesses.

Artie pokes his head out and says, "It's 'jumping frogs.'" Then he takes the jug and passes it to unseen hands within the tent, and then turns back to me and grabs the cups. "Thanks, Debbie," he says, which I think is polite of him to remember to say.

Two heaping bowls of popcorn sit on the kitchen countertop ready for the boys, and some for us in the house, too. Back outside I flit with this bounty.

"Jumping frogs," I say, expecting a friendly response.

A voice floats out from the inner sanctum: "That's wrong!" followed by gales of laughter.

"That's what you said it was!" I yelp indignantly, and set the bowl on the ground so that I can scratch at a mosquito bite on my leg.

"We had to change it because spies figured out the first one," Jimmy tells me.

"That's no fair! Now, give me the new one, or I'm telling on you guys!" My voice splinters with fury. "Besides, I have popcorn and I'm going straight back in the house with it! So there!" I augment sulkily, as I strike an unseen pose of leaving.

"Wait! Come on, Debbie, want to see inside?" Artie asks solicitously, his coonskin cap sitting askew because he's thrust his head out with lightning speed.

*Boy, oh boy! Do I ever!* I exclaim silently; but I keep my own counsel, as I don't want to appear desperately anxious.

Once inside I hand over the heaping bowl and locate a seat suitable for perusing the interior. I try to appear blasé about my survey, while the boys stuff popcorn into their greedy mouths--I am not feeling very charitable toward them for making me suffer. A heavy flashlight dangles from a central loop and gives the space a peculiar orange smudginess. Sleeping bags hide the floor and comics complete the littered, untidy space . . . there's nothing intriguing here, not a single scrap of good information to convey to Becky. And furthermore, the ghost story Jacky regales us with is corny and trite, so . . .

"See you. I'm going in." I yawn, crawling backward out through the opening.

Once in bed, I comfort myself with the revelation that not one single fascinating matter is occurring outside in our backyard tent. "Pooh! Who cares, anyway?"

In the morning, watching Mom at the sewing machine in Artie's bedroom, I take pleasure in picturing the mess in the backyard. It's sure to take the boys most of the morning to straighten things up. Ha, ha!

"Mom, is this mine or Becky's school dress?" I ask, fingering the soft wool fabric she's working with.

"This is Becky's. Yours is the green-and-blue plaid in the sack on the bed," she tells me with pins between her lips.

I draw the fabric from the bag along with a pattern that shows a girl skipping rope in a jumper. "I like it." I smile dreamily. "Mom, who do you guess my teacher will be this year?" Imagining my new teacher consumes a considerable amount of my attention as the first day of school draws within sight.

"Oh, I don't know." She's concentrating intensely on her task, so the pause is prolonged. Then she pushes away from the machine and looks at me. "Let's see, Becky had Mrs. Barter in third grade, didn't she? You might get her, or maybe Mrs. Ross. Both are exceptional teachers."

--People came to Climax from all over the U.S.A., many of them talented and well educated. The stock of teachers was undeniably premier. The great majority of the adult residents were in their twenties and thirties in the mid-1950s. There was, for example, a capable man, Leo Fondacaro, who lived in camp for a couple of years with his wife and young son. They were from New York City and happened to be avid patrons of the opera. Fondacaro had been hired to work for the Recreation Department, under Hy Gordon. Their son, Roland, was in Becky's class; Mom gave him day care for a short time. Roland, who had quite a pronounced eastern accent, would entertain us by singing opera from atop a flat boulder platform. We felt ourselves very fortunate, indeed, to be handed this source of amusing entertainment, sitting on the ground beside the makeshift stage, knowing absolutely nothing about opera, let alone New York City.

The original founders of the mine were probably of the entrepreneurial and adventure-seeking mold; however, each of the subsequent presidents of the Company, Jack White, Max Schott, Brainerd Phillipson, and Arthur Stork, were highly educated and were experts in mining and mining engineering. Later successors were, likewise, mining engineers in one capacity or another. Because of this, Climax was able to lure a remarkable breed of people to her mountain during the decades from 1930 to the 1960s, people who stayed and raised families and who added allure, sophistication, and spark to the community. People of stamina, imagination, and the vigor of youth.—

All during my growing-up years Mom made most of our clothes: dresses, skirts, blouses, and frothy organdy dresses for church. Shoot. She even made a few suits for Artie. She can sew just like a professional, and is self-taught. As often as not, when we come in from playing outside we find her at the sewing machine. Each of us is fond of visiting with her as she sews. The piles of fabric, remnants, and garments-in-progress--she often works on more than one project at a time--are comforting to have about, but because the clutter keeps Artie's room in disarray, he doesn't have to worry about making it tidy, like Becky and I do. Humph!

Mom is resourceful and sews patches on our jeans when we get holes in the knees. Seems like Artie wears patched pants exclusively, which is why Becky and I get such a kick out of teasing him and calling him "Patches." He becomes quite livid when we incite him with this nickname, too, which just makes it more fun.

Once when Artie and I were home alone, Mom was next door visiting with Arlene Prier, for some reason I was in a downright devilish and mean-spirited mood, so I taunted him relentlessly. "Oh, Patches, you look so elegant." "Patches, may I touch one of your delicate patches?" And, "I wish my clothes were covered in chic patches, too, Patches." And on and on, until Artie exploded, like the Big Blast, and began chasing me from room to room until I skidded around a corner and skinned my knee. The chase resumed in earnest with me in tears, but then he stumbled against the end table by the couch and the lamp crashed to the floor in a zillion pieces—which certainly dampened our spirits considerably. The consequences included one week of extra chores and, the worst part, no playing with friends! Art and I tried our best not to get into skirmishes for quite a while, but this did try our patience, like Mom is always saying to us. "Now, don't try my patience," she says, when we're horsing around and not minding her.

# Chapter Eight

*The child sits on the ground surrounded by an array of dolls and stuffed animals. She meticulously lines them up side by side forming two neat columns, and leans back to carefully study the arrangement. She speaks sternly to them in a make-believe adult voice, warning them not to move, or in any way shift out of order; then she leaves them, knowing that they will obey her commands in her absence.*

--One of the ways that the Climax Recreation Hall helped families cope with nine months of harsh winter weather was to provide a showplace for movies. Twice a week the gym became a movie theater and ran classic films, as well as current first-run films. Volunteer junior high boys set up chairs facing a stage from which hung voluminous dark-blue velvet curtains, and when the curtains opened a projectionist rolled the film onto a giant screen. Popcorn, sodas, and candy were sold at a portable concession counter, which made going to the movies as popular in the Climax camp as it was anywhere in the nation.--

Sometimes when I join my best friends, Bobbie and Rosemary, at the Rec Hall movies, we sprawl on our coats on the floor along with dozens of other little kids in front of the rows of chairs. Peeping at the older kids sitting on seats entertains us immensely, especially when we observe a boy attempting to put an arm around his girlfriend. At times such a display sends us into gales of laughter. Watching the picture show from such an angle causes severe neck discomfort and weariness, though, so the choice of where to sit is a seriously big one.

The following dramatic dialogue plays in my head throughout the movie, *Tarantula*: Scrunched down in my seat, I hold my coat over my head. "Yikes! Look out, lady! The giant tarantula is looking right in your bedroom window! Oh, no! It's going to sit on top of your house, and you'll get squished! Oh, now it's going after the scientist, and . . . yuck! It *ate* him!" My heart's in my throat, and I'm crunching on Atomic Fire Balls, one right after another, so my tongue is really on fire. "Okay. Now the cops and the doctor try to blow up the tarantula on the highway with dynamite. Doesn't work; he's still coming. Here come the fighter planes, just as the giant insect gets to the outskirts of town; the planes drop all kinds of bombs down, and burn the living daylights outta that darned old giant tarantula!"

Walking home after *Tarantula* with the Ducharme boys, streetlights illuminate the road and keep us from stumbling into hideous monsters that might be lurking in shadows. No shortcuts for us, huh-uh!

"Whew! That was the most bloodcurdling movie ever, huh, you guys?" Becky says, awestruck.

"Yeah, it was really cool when those planes flew over an' dropped bombs!" Artie says, and he, Jacky and Jimmy start dive-bombing around us, making airplane noises.

Then they start machine-gunning us girls, making us dart about on the road.

"Remember last week when we saw *Abbot and Costello Meet the Mummy?*" I ask, desiring a change of mindset for the last part of our walk home.

"Oh, yeah. Old Bud Abbot says, 'Is that your mummy?'" Jacky remembers, tickled.

"Yeah. And then Lou Costello says, 'It's not my mummy. Is it your mummy?'" Artie adds giggling.

"Yeah, and then Abbot gives him a whack!" Jimmy laughs, and we are bonded, momentarily, by a collective giddiness.

The whistle blows. The nine o'clock curfew whistle! To be out past the curfew is tempting fate, and courting disaster in our juvenile minds. Trepidation envelops us like a shroud.

"Watch out for the paddy wagon!" Jimmy cautions needlessly. Heads swivel, all ears and eyes straining to penetrate the sinister void surrounding us.

"What if they discover us out here in the dead of night?" I moan, inclined to unleash a torrent of tears.

"Yeah. Why don't you just start blubbering, like you always do?" Jimmy asks.

"Don't you start hassling my sister, if you know what's good for you," Becky hisses in a whispery voice.

"Don't worry," he says, "I won't."

His admission makes my insides balmy with a blissful butterfly fluttering. Silently I rejoice, in spite of our pressing plight. *Jimmy's not going to pester me! Yippee! We're all too scared that the guards will ensnare us to waste energy squabbling, I guess.*

"Here they come!" Artie shrieks, just as we get to within spitting distance of our driveway. And he's right: the paddy wagon progresses down 10th Street and passes our house. We holler, "'Bye, you guys!" and flash into the secure haven of home, where Mom and Dad whisk us off to bed without a flicker of fanfare.

--As previously mentioned, the War Department was very concerned about possible sabotage at the Climax Molybdenum Company because molybdenum, a steel-strengthening agent, had become very important to the war effort. A steel-mesh fence, topped by four rows of barbed wire, encircled the entire camp. During WWII, the guards were commissioned by the War Department to carry weapons and act as soldiers when patrolling the Company's perimeters. They routinely scouted around the areas that were not fenced in, such as the tailing ponds and the water pipes running into the mill. And to repeat, it was the war years that necessitated the procedure of prohibiting all but Climax employees, and their families, entrance into camp. The Korean War and the Cold War dictated a comparable degree of vigilance.

Hence, the Climax Protection Department remained a steadfast part of camp life from the very early days until the last. For instance, during the '50s, the Protection Department attended to keeping peace and order inside the camp's community. The guards, numbering around twenty during this time, rotated on the same shifts that governed the lives of everyone employed by Climax. They drove about camp in vehicles equipped with two-way radios, one being a 1953 panel truck, referred to as a paddy wagon. Truly, if ever a prisoner needed transporting, the guards would be all set up to transport him to the jail located in the guardhouse.

The paddy wagon was also necessary and indispensable for use as an ambulance. There were some weeks when, as often as two or three times a day, the guards would be summoned to the mine to pick up a sick or injured miner, and then transport him to Climax Hospital. On a few tragic occasions, the guards had to recover a dead miner. In such an event, they would bear the victim to the hospital, where the death pronouncement was made, and then the Leadville mortuary people would come into camp and take over the procedures.

Tom McAuliffe was Chief Guard during the '50s, and, the support his guard force provided around camp not withstanding, it was keeping the unruly school-aged children in line that routinely kept the guards occupied. They also settled minor public or domestic disputes, supplied transportation to the hospital for residents in case of illness or accident, and were in charge of the fire engines.

Darrell Stewart, a Climax guard for twenty-seven years, and Chief Guard when he retired, related an amusing story about a fellow guard. The guard, Tex Rucker, drove up past Ryan's Camp on a road that passed alongside the Glory Hole in order to check on a gate into Climax property. Rucker left his vehicle running while he examined the gate. As he turned back around, he watched in absolute horror and disbelief as his vehicle rolled backward down into the Glory Hole . . . In short order, the dun-colored G.I. Dodge power wagon was replaced with another, a '55 Chevy station wagon, but alas, the paddy wagon *we* loved to fear had met with its demise.

The whistle we heard at various times during each twenty-four-hour day had evolved over the course of time. The first to be used was a three-inch brass bell, and had to be blown manually. Next, a five-inch brass whistle bell was kept in the steam plant. And finally, a whistle in the compressor room was blown on a timer. These various whistles signaled the shift changes: day, swing and graveyard. The whistle blew at noon, and at the 9:00 PM curfew hour. The whistle would be used in the eventuality of an air raid. Climax built a state-of-the-art bomb shelter inside the mine when such sites were deemed necessary. The shelter was spacious and stocked so that it could accommodate all the residents of Lake County. And it was the fire alarm, which could be heard from as far away as the nearby 14'ers (Democrat, Lincoln and Bross). There was a much smaller version in place at the Phillipson portal, which signaled the miners that trains were going into and out of the mine. And, last but not least, the whistle was blown in the mine before and during a Big Blast explosion underground. So it was the guards, the paddy wagon, and the curfew whistle that, singly or combined, personified the boogieman to Climax kids.--

Today is Saturday, and Mom pronounced at breakfast that we must clean our room before going outside to play.

"Hey, Debbie, guess what?" Becky asks, as she yanks the sheets from her bed.

From the closet floor where our laundry has amassed, I answer, "What?"

"Anna Vierling told me about some boys that the guards were chasing over around the sand piles. And guess what? Those boys had been caught right in the act of climbing the water tower!"

I pause from tucking the sheet in on my bed, and glance over at her. "That's pretty dumb! Who are the boys, anyway?"

"One is Danny McAuliffe and the other is Rusty Brewer. And guess what?"

"What?" I ask, becoming fairly interested, even though I don't know the boys, and sit on her freshly made bed.

"Get off of my bed," she says before continuing. "Mr. McAuliffe was one of the guards who was chasing them!"

Wide-eyed with wonder, I step to the window and stare out. "Ho! Is he going to kick his own boy out of camp?"

--Although I never once saw a "black book," one reportedly did exist. The story went that any kid who was ornery and mischievous enough to get his name recorded three times or more in the black book the guards carried, would be kicked out of camp. My sister, brother and I were young and unaware of the capers of older kids. But, by nature of the age, twelve- and thirteen-year-olds were a handful for the guards.

Two boys in particular made a game of outwitting the guards on a regular basis: Danny McAuliffe and Rusty Brewer. Using a Y-shaped piece of pine and strips of car tire inner tube rubber, the two fashioned slingshots they called "beanie shooters," hard beans being the ammunition. Small stones worked as well, and were likely more readily available than beans.

Armed with their handmade weapons, the two would wage war on squirrels and sparrows in the woods, as well as on other kids and each other. They actually used the beanie shooters to break windows in some industrial buildings. The guards would give chase when the boys were out and about camp wreaking havoc. Danny, Rusty, and their friends took great pleasure in outfoxing their pursuers, of course. On one occasion, the boys attempted to climb the black water tower that was used as the industrial water supply. Aided by binoculars, the guards spotted the juveniles, and the chase was on. The boys led the guards on a merry chase around a variety of Company buildings, and up through Ryan's Camp across the multi-acre lot of sand/gravel piles used in mixing concrete in the mine, and finally, into the woods above the apartment buildings on Timberline Street, where the two youths found sanctuary.

The lads, though, were dissatisfied with their victories unless they could brag about their successes to the Chief Guard, namely, Danny's dad, Tom McAuliffe. In fact, some evenings the boys would actually draw out a diagram of a chase on the McAuliffe kitchen blackboard, and then demonstrate to the Chief how they had ditched his guard force during the day.

Nevertheless, the guards were far from comical Keystone Cops, and because the Protection Department employed as many as twenty-five men, there was enough time and manpower most days that their routine duties included keeping kids from causing any real damage to themselves or Company property.

Lastly, the guardhouse did contain a jail with an iron door that was put into use only a few times. Once, Guard Darrell Stewart had to lock up the Lykins boys for disorderly behavior, driving around the streets of camp a bit crazily. Stewart called Ray Lykins, their father, to tell him about the boys and to see if he wanted to come and get them, but Lykins said just to keep them locked up overnight.—

My imagination is whirling and spinning around, as the story Becky has just told me plays out in my head. I'm quite overcome with awe at the notion that kids would dare to tweak the nose of authority. And, the boldness of the boys prying open the jaws of jeopardy, simply as a lark, is completely beyond my ability to comprehend.

At length it occurs to me to ask, "How come Anna knew about the boys being chased by the guards?" We're sitting on the floor ridding our bookcase of old magazines and clutter.

"Cuz on our way home from the Rec Hall yesterday, Thomas Stevens, Marilyn Dickeson, and I, were sitting on the school steps with Jill Brown, so she could rest for a while before starting to her house over on Third Street. We were just sitting there when Anna came along on her bike, and she sat down with us, and told the entire story, okay? Anna said that her sisters were talking about it the other night when they were coming back from the movie. And, Anna's sister, Tia, just happens to be best friends with Danny McAuliffe's girlfriend. But don't ask me what her name is, because I don't know."

Becky continues flipping the pages of an old *Life* magazine, but from the vacant look in her eyes, she seems completely preoccupied. After a time she remarks, "But it's no big deal, because they didn't get kicked out of camp." And as a final afterthought, she adds with furrowed brow, "I wish Jimmy Ducharme would get kicked out of camp, don't you?"

# Chapter Nine

*Education--so much has been said about how important it is for a child to get a good one. The little girl flaps her arms up and down, pretending to be a barnyard fowl, as she chants, "Cock a doodle do! The rooster says to you, 'Wake up boys and girls! Its time to go to school!'" And then, skipping around in circles, the child sings, "School days, school days, good old Golden Rule days!" As she sings, she wonders what a "Golden Rule" is. She'll have to remember to ask.*

--At that time, C.D. Snyder was the superintendent of Max Schott School, and Rick Cosseboom was the principal of grades kindergarten through twelve. Mr. Cosseboom didn't unsettle kids by his manner and appearance, but Mr. Snyder, although rather slight of stature, put the fear of God into my friends and me. When Mr. Snyder ventured into my classroom to have a look around I would hunker down in my desk, so that he couldn't penetrate me with his glowering gaze. This, of course, was my childish perception.

The Max Schott School was accredited before it even opened its doors for the first time, in large part because of the professional staff, as well as the high-quality facility. The teachers were wholly competent and professional; the students were fortunate to have such a high-caliber staff to educate them. When the first wave of Baby Boomers ballooned the school enrollment to 657 in 1956, the majority in the elementary grades, three teachers taught the third grade, Mrs. Ross, Mrs. Dryden, and Mrs. Yanish.—

"Hey, Mom, I got Mrs. Ross!" I'm breathless from sprinting the last part home.

"Well, that's wonderful, DoGo. Do you happen to know who Becky got?" Mom asks me, as she takes the dinner rolls from the oven. Her yeast rolls are a mouth-watering sensation, and the flavorful aroma now floats about the kitchen.

"I don't know, I didn't see her because the fifth graders go out for recess after us. Who did Artie get?" I ask. She took Artie to school so he wouldn't be scared on his first day of first grade; Becky and I walked with our friends.

"Mrs. Avants. And he did just fine after he saw Jacky and Joe." My eyes follow her movements as she lifts fried chicken pieces from the skillet. "I guess we'll have to wait for your sister to get home to find out who her teacher is, hmm?"

And just then, Becky sails through the back door.

"Hi, sweetheart. Who's your teacher this year?" Mom asks, drying her hands on a dishtowel.

"Mrs. Monk. She seems pretty nice, so far. Anna Vierling and Marilyn Dickeson are both in my class, and so is Jill Brown." She drops into a chair.

"Rosemary and Bobbie both got Mrs. Ross, too!" I suddenly remember, and jig around the room.

"Well, isn't that nice? You girls set the table before your dad gets home from work."

Us Vincent kids adore school. We never miss a single day, unless we catch something that makes us sick as a dog, which did happen late last spring when Artie and I both caught the Asian flu. We didn't even get into scuffles or arguments because we were so sick with fever, and coughing our heads off. It was a miserable two whole weeks before we got well.

Oh, yeah, and when we got the chicken pox Mom had sick kids underfoot for a month, because we passed it from one to the other. But, that time none of us felt very sick, so we spent the days horsing around, roughing each other up, and sprawling around the living room, watching cartoons. Mom was very glad to see the last of those spots, she said.

We use basically the same shortcut to get to Max Schott School as we did going to and from Sister School except we turn at 6th and onto Lake Street, the street the school is on. Once the snow starts piling up, though, we're forbidden to take shortcuts, which we hate, because streets use up so much time. But, unreasonable as it seems, we always try to mind Mom about her shortcut obsession, so that she won't be anxious.

Max Schott School has two stories; the junior high and the high school levels are on the top floor, and on the bottom are the other grades, kindergarten to sixth grade. My class has a nice big cloakroom where we stow all of our stuff, like coats, boots, mittens, and snow pants. A radiator stands against the wall in the classroom, where at times we arrange our mittens to dry out. When all those soggy mittens are spitting and melting water to the floor, the room gets thick with wet-wool smell, but I like it.

Snow pants are a significant bother for girls to wear to school. If I tuck my dress, petticoats and crinolines into them, I look like a stuffed teddy bear, and walking with such bulk around my legs is awkward. I can leave my dress hanging outside the pants, but if I do, by the time I get to school the dress and under things have snowballs dangling from them, and I don't dry out for half the morning. One way or the other, wearing snow pants to school is no pleasure for girls.

All the kids in the lower grades eat lunch in the cafeteria first, then it's the bigger kids' turn. Sometimes on real snowy days we take our time to eat, instead of rushing right outside, and if we linger long enough, a particular pair of high school girls supply us with some worthwhile entertainment. Bobbie, Rosemary, and I laugh and whisper around those two older girls until they get fed up, lose their tempers, and tell us to "Scat!" which we do very quickly, like mischievous puppies.

One day when I get to school Bobbie meets me in the cloakroom, where I'm getting out of my outdoor gear.

"Guess what today is, Debbie?" Bobbie is always up to one thing or another, so I don't leap into venturing a hasty guess. By the time I've wiggled and wrestled my shoes out of my boots, I've figured out what the day's cheerless affair is. "I know--it's shots, right?"

She nods her head sagaciously, but then giggles as we saunter into the classroom. "Remember last year, when Joe Carmody just slipped to the floor after his shot, like a saggy old rag doll, or something?"

"Yeah, and then everybody behind him in line got all agitated and anxious. And, remember Patsy Phelps fainted next, and it wasn't even her turn for four people!" I added, covering my nervous giggles with my hand.

"I hate shots," Bobbie admits seriously, with a puckered brow.

"Me, too. But, you know . . . Jill Brown . . ." I remind my friend solemnly.

--Jill Brown was a good friend of Becky's who, having been stricken with infantile polio, wore braces on her legs, and used crutches. Polio was a colossal concern in those days, and because of Jill Brown, we kids had sound evidence that the threat of polio was bona fide, and that vaccinations were not a ruse used for torturing kids, simply to prevent some unlikely misfortune. Along with the polio vaccine, we were also given booster shots to guard against an entire range of diseases, smallpox included. The nurses from the Climax Hospital came directly to the school to give us the shots, which ensured that all the children, not just a smattering, were inoculated.—

"I hope our class gets called right away, so we don't have to wait, don't you?" Bobbie says as we walk into the classroom.

"Yeah." I park myself down at my desk.

Just then a boy with dishwater-blonde hair falling over his eyebrows, Francis Gill, enters the room, ambles deliberately down my row, and places a paper on my desktop. I grimace, jerking my face to the windows, as the blood rushes hotly into my head. I blink rapidly to disperse the salsa stars, and have to swallow hastily to dispel the juices that threaten to gurgle past my throat and into my mouth. Oh, how I deplore his public pronouncements that I am his girlfriend. I am not. All of my friends know that I shudder whenever he gets near me. I know it's unkind, but he shuffles in shoes with the backs mashed under his heels, and sometimes his hands have crusty dirt on them. Yuck!

So, as I struggle for composure, I hazard a glance at the paper that sits on my desktop, staring up at me. The pitiful offering is a drawing of a boy and a girl strolling hand in hand by a house. Oh dear. I sense that he's watching my every move, so I warily remove last week's *Weekly Reader* from inside my desk, and use it to conceal his childish illustration, figuring that I'll toss it in the wastebasket at the earliest opportunity.

Eventually, about halfway through the morning, Mrs. Ross instructs us to line up for shots. Her announcement generates sensations akin to those caused earlier by Francis Gill--fluttery stomach, and mouth flooding with hot, thick wetness. I queue up at the end of line between Stephanie Valerio and Donald Wilson, which happens every single time, because of my name beginning with V. Our line snakes up the stairs to the station where nurses are serving up shots like there's no tomorrow. Cries from a few younger kids float down to us, adding to the dreadfulness of the entire experience. Waiting in line leaves us hushed and gloomy, like trapped laboratory mice with no escaping the cage. The line inches forward gradually, relentlessly delivering me nearer to the inevitable sting and misery.

At last, my turn arrives and I must remove my navy-blue sweater, so that the nurse can poke the needle into my exposed tender skin. I try tremendously to be brave, but when that smelly hospital cotton is swiped over my arm, my eyes flood with tears, and I whimper, "Ouch!" And then it's all over.

One day Rosemary and I are walking home from school on the short cut path between the houses just above 5th Street, because it hasn't snowed for two solid weeks, so the trail has hardly any snow pack on it and I ask her, "What are you going to the Halloween Carnival as?" I'm carrying three library books, along with my unnecessary coat and scarf, as lately a measure of Indian summer has been bestowed on Climax.

As she's ahead of me, she halts and turns. "I think a witch again, or maybe a ghost."

"Mom's making me a gypsy costume. Usually I go as a ghost; for the last three years that's what I've been. Start walking, or we'll never get home."

"I'm going, hold your horses! You're a lucky duck dressing up as a gypsy! Should we meet at the carnival?"

"Oh, yes, let's do." And precisely at this moment, two boys jump out from behind a garage that butts up against the path. One boy grabs my arms to keep me from running, and just that quickly, Francis Gill swoops in like a chicken hawk and kisses me right on my cheek! Oh! Oh! Oh! I burst into tears, and the boys run off.

Rosemary puts her arm around my shoulder, her face crinkled with concern. My books and coat are strewn around, so she helps me collect everything, all the while attempting to sooth my offended dignity. Presently we get underway, and then I vow, "I will settle scores with that idiotic boy, one way or another, just wait and see."

When I get home Mom is in Artie's room. "What are you sewing, Mom?"

"This is your gypsy costume." She hands me the pattern package, so that I can see what it looks like.

"Oh, neat-o! Is it going to have these same ruffles all up and down the skirt?"

"Uh-huh, just like the pattern."

The stuff she's sewing on appears to be crepe paper. Three colors: orange, green and blue, are lying in heaps all over Artie's bedroom floor. Hmmm.

The Rec Hall gym is decorated lavishly with creepy ghosts, witches, and spidery webs. After strolling around for a while scrutinizing costumed kids, I catch sight of Bobbie and Rosemary over by a booth.

"Hi, you guys!"

"Hey, Debbie, we're going to do the fish pond, okay?" Bobbie squeals, who's disguised as a pirate, eye patch, mustache, and all.

"Okay. How many tickets does it take?" I ask, inspecting my strip of attached tickets.

"Just two," Rosemary tells me. "Come on, let's go." And off we frolic to have fun, but before long, Bobbie and Rosemary spy Francis Gill with his friends, who come racing right over to blemish the evening's merriment.

"Hey, Debbie, want to go to the marriage booth with me, and pretend to get married? They give you a golden ring to wear and everything," Francis asks brashly.

Well, Bobbie and Rosemary crumple up giggling, but my face gets hot as fire, my breathing erratic. I'm finally able to draw in a long, deep breath, and then I exhale slowly. "No, thanks. I'm busy with my friends. So, please, just leave us alone," I say firmly, and then, taking hold of my friends' hands, I race across the gym floor. Oh, boy! Inwardly sighing, I secretly allow that payback time for his unwanted attention is not in the cards, for now.

At long last, it's time for us to parade around the gym in order that the high school kids can judge our costumes. After circumventing the gym at least twice, someone behind me accidentally steps on the bottom ruffles of my dress. Rrripp! The whole bottom part of my skirt ruffles come unraveled and fall to the floor, one row after the other, until I'm left in a dress that comes midway to my knees and waist. Well, that does it! This final disaster spoils everything for me for the remainder of the party.

And to add insult to injury, since the following night is Trick or Treat, I have to go out into the darkness dressed up as a (sheet) ghost, my wonderful gypsy costume nothing now but a sack full of crumpled crepe paper. Boy, oh boy.

--The Recreation Director, Hy Gordon, was from a farming community in eastern Colorado where he had homesteaded with his mother and sister; he was also an auctioneer, traveling far and wide to call the numbers. Unfortunately, his farm was wiped out during the Depression. So he came to Climax with his sons, and worked for the Recreation Department. There were nearly 3000 people in Climax in 1956. Hy Gordon coordinated the dozens of clubs and organizations in camp, which was more than a full-time job, but he had a competent staff helping him out.

Climax had twenty-six organizations, and all of them very active. The list included the American Legion, Boy Scouts, Girl Scouts, Sewing Club, Bridge Club, 4-H Club, Square Dance Club, Hi Homemakers, and Junior Chorus, along with a dozen sports clubs: golf, softball, basketball, boxing, and of course, bowling: twenty men's teams, seventeen women's teams, and twenty-four children's teams. The Recreation Hall had four bowling alleys, as well as a room full of pool tables. Hy Gordon, with his distinctive auctioneer's voice, announced the action over a speaker system during all the Little League and adult softball games at the ball field and because the field was lit with lights, people could even enjoy night games. People in Climax could be as busy and active as they chose to be.—

# Chapter Ten

*A box on a crocheted doily sits atop a cabinet in the living room. The little girl is perched on a stool, directly in front of the highly polished cherry wood box, listening with rapt attention to "Dick Tracy" when the front door opens, and two men in overalls carry in a much, much larger cherry wood box, one with a glass screen on the front; it is placed in the exact location where the first box was sitting. The smaller box is carried into the attic. The little girl sits directly in front of the new box, watching the screen with rapt attention.*

"Hot diggity, dog diggity, boom, what you do to me! It's so new to me, what you do to me! Hot diggity, dog diggity, boom, what you do to me, when you're holding me tight!" I sing and flutter along the street as lighthearted as a bird flying from an open cage on a Saturday morning in early November. Snow is in every breath of air--I can feel its promise on my cheeks, but it's not snowing yet. We've already had some fairly substantial storms: it snowed all day long on my birthday, September 28th, (so now I truly am eight years old) and last week, it snowed without stopping from Sunday to Sunday.

Right now, I'm glad to be on my way to Rosemary Cleeves' down at the very end of 10th Street. I'm tremendously tired of playing with boisterous, bothersome boys and can't wait to spend time with my agreeable friend. Rosemary moved to Climax late last spring, just before summer vacation began, but I didn't get the chance to know her until the tail end of the school year in second grade. Now that she's in my class, we've become bosom buddies, along with Bobbie.

Rosemary has white-blonde hair and a very round face. She giggles a lot, and so do I when we're in each other's company. She has two younger brothers and a little sister, but she dismisses their existence as even being part of the human race. They are too goofy she says, and, naturally I agree with her. Today, she and I are going to walk down to the bowling alleys at the Rec Hall and bowl with our Brownie troop, and maybe have a meeting.

"Want a stick of gum?" Rosemary asks, and takes off a mitten, so that she can divide the stick of Juicy Fruit in half.

"Sure. Yum, my favorite kind. Thanks." I grin sunnily, unselfconscious about my toothless smile; after all she's toothless, too, which makes us two peas in a pod.

The two of us keep shifting gears, walking and running, and walking, again; in no time at all, we reach the Rec Hall and bounce downstairs to the bowling alleys. Our Brownie troop is gathered at one alley, changing into bowling shoes, and being quite loud with all their chattering. Before joining them, we check out bowling shoes for ourselves.

This is already my third time bowling, but I'm not improving very much. I can't seem to get the hang of it--my ball rolls down the gutter every third time or so. Regardless, I whoop it up with my friends, and have heaps of fun, before it's time to go.

The commissary on the first floor of the Recreation Hall is a special place for us to go for candy, ice cream, or soft drinks. You can buy sandwiches, hamburgers, and chili there, too, but we never do. Just candy. I follow Rosemary in there now because we each have money for all-day suckers.

Before we tie on scarves, button coats, and pull on boots and mittens, we gaze out at the heavy fat flakes whirling and swirling, blanketing the earth. We set off, hand in hand, hiking up the steep streets of our mountain home.

In time, my friend's voice splinters the delicate silence of our white world. "Is it going to snow all day, do you think, Debbie?"

"Yeah. And maybe all night, too; lots of times it does." Our breath clouds around our heads during this exchange, and our swinging arms warm my fingertips.

"It never snows in Fallbrook."

"Where's Fallbrook?"

"California. That's where we used to live. It's by the ocean, or kind of close, anyway."

"Oh. Did you like living there?"

"Uh-huh. We'll probably go back to visit when we have our next vacation. My grandparents are taking care of our avocado ranch."

Well, I've never heard of an avocado, so I have to ask, "What's an av'cado? Some kind a animal or something?"

My question ends our handholding, and I step back as Rosemary hoots and cackles until she actually snorts. Her reaction really hurts my feelings. In fact, she continues for so long that I become annoyed with her, and tears begin to pool at the surface of my eyes. "What is so funny?" I demand, over and over, while stomping my feet.

At last, when she can speak without busting up she says, "Avocados are fruit, or maybe, vegetables, silly."

"Humph. Well, you're not so smart, if you don't even know which one--fruit or vegetables. Anyway, we don't eat that kind of stuff in Climax."

"They don't taste that good, anyway," she says, smoothing my ruffled feathers.

After all, we are best friends.

Mom is sewing when I get home from bowling; Dad is doing something out in the garage, and Artie's out there with him.

"Hi, Mom! I'm home. Where's Becky?" I sprawl out on Artie's bed.

"Hi, honey. Becky went to Dillon with the Priers. How was the Brownie meeting?"

"We didn't even have a Brownie meeting, just bowling, and I am entirely rotten at it. My ball just keeps going in the gutter almost every single time. Everyone in our troop was there, except Talca Patton and Barbara Linn. Hey, Mom, know what? Next week's meeting is at Stephanie Valerio's, and we're getting our picture taken, so I have to wear my Brownie uniform. And you know what else? Rosemary says that they used to grow alvocades on a farm, where she lived in California."

"They used to grow what?" Mom asks, and looks up from the sewing machine at me. She's holding pins between her lips, so she takes time to push them into the pincushion before turning back to me.

"Some kind of fruit or vegetable . . . I forget, alcadoes, I think."

"Oh. Avocados." She smiles and turns back to her sewing.

"Yeah, that's it. I said we don't eat those things in Climax. Do we, Mom?"

"Well, the stores don't stock them very often, although I've seen them in Safeway from time to time. Would you like to try one sometime, DoGo?"

"Oh, yes, I really would; that would be stupendous!" Then I just loll there watching her for a while. "What're you making, Mom?" The fabric she's sewing on looks like soft clouds, and the color reminds me of cantaloupe, a fruit that does appeal to me.

"Oh, this is a dress I'm making for myself to wear to the Cloud Club dinner on Saturday. I'm having a dickens of a time with this netting that attaches to the skirt, though," she says, puckering her forehead.

"Well, it looks pretty, so far. So, Mom, does that mean that we're getting a sitter?" I ask hopefully, scooting off the bed.

"Uh-huh."

"Goody, Mom!" And I embrace the back of her, as she sits at the machine. "Can I turn on the TV set, and see if the 'Fred and Fay Show' is on?"

"You can try, but your father mentioned that the reception wasn't coming in this morning."

--Late in May of 1953, some men who worked at Climax had the notion to snowshoe up the ridge on 13,770-foot Mt. McNamee, the highest point on Ceresco Ridge that connects to Mt Bartlett, to see if they could get television signals from Denver on their equipment. Once on the summit, they found that they were, indeed, able to receive signals, so they got the Company to agree to pay for the project. It was a complicated and arduous undertaking, but by August several volunteers had erected a shelter to house a signal amplifier and the large antenna on Mt. McNamee's summit. They ran the cable wires right down the face of Mt Bartlett into the mine, and out through the Phillipson portal. Every miner took great pains to keep the television cable wires that ran through the mine from getting damaged.

In no time at all, the maintenance crews installed television antenna leads to the individual houses in camp. Climax became the first town in central Colorado to get TV because of the efforts of a handful of daring men with a vision. We bought an RCA television down at the Fremont Trading Post right away. It was a bulky mahogany console that took up a third of one living room wall, a place of honor. It's amazing to think of it now, but the screen was a mere seven inches wide.—

We almost always have hotcakes and eggs for supper on Friday nights, and Dad says we do this because we're mackerel snappers. And every Friday after supper, Dad loves to watch a boxing program, "Friday Night Fights," and he ritually drinks a chocolate milkshake while he watches it.

On Saturday mornings Becky, Artie, and I like watching "The Howdy Doody Show" with that idiotic Clara Bell, and right after that, "The Cisco Kid." We laugh until tears roll down our cheeks at Poncho and Cisco, and the way they talk. Like this: "Hey, Pon-cho!" "Hey, Ceesco! Ah eiiee!" And sometimes, when we get home from school we watch "The Fred and Fay Show." "The Mickey Mouse Club" is a first-rate program for after-school viewing, but Saturday morning is the absolute unsurpassed kids' show time. "The Lone Ranger" comes on just before "Roy Rogers and Dale Evens," and finally, "Lassie." Then we go outside to play.

I turn on the set right now, but it's just the test pattern . . . not entertaining by any stretch of the imagination. So, outside I go to see if anyone's around to play with. Nope, nary a living soul. I stomp down on the snow under the eaves of the roof in the front yard, so that I can practice playing jacks--I have an old bath mat spread out on this flattened area--when the Priers pull up next door. They all tumble out of the station wagon, including Becky, who zooms in to where I'm sitting on my snowy rug.

"Did you have fun down in Dillon?" I ask her, bouncing the ball for "foursies."

"Okay, I guess. Not so much, though," she tells me, turning toward the house.

"How's come?" I ask, trying to delay her from going inside for a while. You never know, she just might agree to play jacks.

"Nothing to do down there, that's how come."

--In those days, before skiing became a lucrative industry, Summit County towns like Dillon, Frisco, and Breckenridge, were mere hamlets.

There was no Vail, no Copper Mountain, no Keystone, and in fact, no Lake Dillon to supply the Front Range with water. In those days, the villages were tiny populations of folks who ran hunting lodges, or maybe small shops and markets to supply fishermen and other outdoorsmen. Very few tourists came to the central Colorado mountain area before the ski resorts and the Interstate were built, because mountain roads were quite hazardous, even in the summer months, and not many people were fearless or adventurous enough to risk driving the high-country roads.

The route we used traveling to Denver during the wintertime went over Loveland Pass, which in winter would often have to be closed while road crews cleared the highway of avalanches coming down from the Seven Sisters, notorious avalanche runs. Pshaw! Snowstorms and blizzards were commonplace in Climax nine months of the year, and weather conditions never dictated whether or not Climax people chose to go Denver, or wherever. And furthermore, no one owned a four-wheel drive vehicle for getting around. Tire chains, yes, always.–

I've known another of my best friends, Bobbie Middleton, since kindergarten. She makes me giggle a lot, too, like Rosemary. Sometimes on a Friday or Saturday we have sleepovers at each other's houses. Last time, when I was at her house down on Bartlett Street, we played a game called "Cootie," and we laughed our heads off until Lee Middleton, her dad, told us to pipe down for at least the zillionth time.

Her dog's name is Blackie, a fire-engine dog, white with black spots. He always likes to jump up on me; but I'm not familiar with dogs, so I don't care for old Blackie jumping up on me. Bobbie thinks it's hilarious when he does this. On one of my visits she got the idea to force Blackie to play dress up, because we were dressed up as famous, well-heeled singers. We put a raggedy dress and a ridiculous straw hat on Blackie, which made the poor dog look like a daft scarecrow, but he wasn't too keen on having clothes on him, so he hurtled himself around the living room knocking into furniture, the chairs and coffee tables, until he collided with one table, smashing Bobbie's mom's favorite porcelain figurine to the floor. And all the time we kept racing after poor, distraught Blackie, trying to tackle him, but we couldn't gain purchase. Miriam Middleton came to see what the racket was all about, so I decided to get myself on home, a grueling uphill hike, before Bobbie's mom had a chance to blow her top.

When I am walking home from anywhere my head is awash in imagining and make-believe. One preferred daydream is to fantasize that I'm a dancer wearing a twirling, gossamer dress on a brightly lit stage, leaping and pirouetting to music in my head. To an onlooker it probably looks like I've gone completely insane and lost my marbles, but because I totally lack self-consciousness, I don't give a thought to how strange my behavior might appear.

Mentally I spin through space and into the stories about places in far-off lands that we've been studying in school. Today I'm riding on a camel through the desert, but a dust storm disorients me, until, at last, I see a sparkling white city in the distance, but alas, it's a mirage. I thrash my camel into a frenzied gallop, as I've a terrible thirst, having become dazzled and spellbound by sand and sun. My long flowing robes, my unfastened coat, whip out and around my camel. Suddenly my head floods with the lyrics of my favorite song, "Whip crack away, whip crack away, whip crack away!" Wait! Whatever can I be thinking? This stagecoach song is completely unsuitable for this present daydream. But before I realize it, I'm at the back door calling out, "I'm home, Mom!" and wondering why I'm so thirsty.

Naturally, Bobbie and I spend hours together playing "Let's pretend." Once at my house a game went like this: Bobbie's turn is first, as she is my guest, and she says, "Let's pretend . . . that we're on a desert island, and we have to build a boat so we can escape." We need something to make the boat out of, so we use the coffee table in my living room. We turn it upside down and slide it down the hallway into my bedroom. Then I take a tablecloth from the china cabinet to use for a boat roof, making a colossal mistake by stretching the cloth and anchoring it tautly under the bed legs, and as we plop on top of it . . . r-r-r-r-rip! Jeepers! Mom's face darkens with storm clouds when she discovers her heirloom all in ruins. Bobbie decides to get herself right on home after that happens, just like I do when the two of us land ourselves in trouble at her house.

Just before bedtime on Saturday evenings, Mom winds my hair on curlers. Lots of times I'm just so drowsy that I fall fast asleep perched on the toilet seat. Becky has naturally curly hair inherited from my dad and his mother. Artie has curly hair, too, but he always gets a crew cut, so it's nothing to him. On the other hand, here I am stuck with straight-as-string hair that has to be put in curlers, which I utterly scorn. And, by the way, this personal feature provides a source for one of my nicknames, "Stringy."

On this Saturday night, I am positioned on the toilet seat lid, getting my hair wound on curlers, which gives me an opportunity to ask Mom some things. "Mom, do you think that a boy should run up and kiss someone without permission?"

She pauses and looks into my eyes thoughtfully before she responds. "Everyone has the right to speak up for herself, when she feels she's been wronged. And also, each of us has privacy rights, including the privacy of our bodies."

"Well, Francis Gill did kiss me without asking, and it makes me so furious, and I think that he ought to be punished!" I keep wadding my shirttail into a ball as I sit there.

She sighs and continues with the curlers. "If this boy kissed you, Debbie, and you had no chance to first say its okay, then he might lack good judgement, but it doesn't make him a bad person. Sometimes we have to swallow our pride and forgive someone, if no real harm's been done. Will you think about this, before you determine to hurt the boy's feelings in some way?" she asks, just as she finishes with my hair.

"Okay, Mom, I'll think about it some more." And I go to bed struggling with her wisdom.

# Chapter Eleven

*The little girl's world is now deeply blanketed with snow, a wonderland of white. If she had forgotten to bring a toy inside before the snows began in earnest, the toy would be unrecoverable for many long months. Unforgotten summer toys do not concern the child, because for now she only has thoughts about her wintertime toys: skis, skates, and sleds. All toys have a season and a there's time for every season under heaven.*

Saturday has rolled around again, and right after breakfast, we set out to ice skate with our friends down at the rink, because skating promises to be of utmost amusement. We bundle up in parkas, scarves, mittens, and boots, and with our skates slung over our shoulders, we head out, Artie, Becky, and I. It snowed twenty-four inches the past two days, but this morning the sky is deepest azure, so blue that if I close my eyes, and then open them quickly, I'm able to trigger the sensation of soaring into the sky. Bright sun striking ultra-white snow causes us to squint our eyes into thin slits.

On this splendid day, walking on the snow-packed road down to the end of 10th Street is boastfully satisfying. All of us habitually eat fresh fallen snow; right now it melts rapidly on my hot tongue, and then cools my throat, refreshingly.

"I wish we coulda brought the sled, then we could zip down to the skating rink like a flashing star," I say, my snow pants hampering a fluid stride.

"Yeah, but you know we aren't allowed to, huh?" Becky says around a mouthful of snow.

"Yeah, I know. Do you guys know what Sharon Shriver said during school recess?"

They both shake their heads no.

"Well, Sharon said that a boy, Kenny Balltrip, I think, was sledding down on White Avenue fast as a speeding bullet, and Sharon said that he was riding the sled on his stomach, and that he sledded right underneath a car that was parked at the hotel annex! He got hurt kind of bad, too, a broken arm, and he had to stay overnight at the clinic."

"Yeah, and that's just precisely the reason that we aren't allowed," Becky reminds us needlessly.

"I know. But I sure do wish we could, anyways," my brother laments, expressing the desire of every Climax kid.

--Something like Sharon's near-disaster story did occur at least once each winter. Not surprising considering, after all, that we did live on the world's prime sledding hill. All 8.5 miles of streets in camp were snow-packed and slick, and virtually every kid in camp owned a sled. Thinking about this now, it's quite astonishing that no one was ever terribly injured, or even worse, killed; although kids did sustain scrapes, cuts, or broken bones at times as the result of a car/sled collision. A note of interest: In bold print in the pamphlet titled "Rules and Regulations" issued by the Protection Department it states: "School-aged children are not allowed to ski or sled on Climax streets." Skiing/sledding was confined to the upper/lower ends of the contractor's road, and in front of Vista Drive leading into the playground.—

Given the edict against sledding, we jerkily slide and glide in our rubber snow boots down Mineral Street, under the train trestle, and on down White Avenue. By the time we're on Haley Street, a very steep street, we laugh uproariously about silly nonsense. Everything we say and do fills us right up with laughing, because it's just this happy kind of day.

"Hey, you guys, I'm king of the mountain! Watch!" Artie says as he scales the mammoth snow bank that edges the road and teeters there, six-year-old tall.

--The Surface Maintenance Crews plowed snow in Climax twenty-four hours a day throughout the nine-month winters. These men kept the snowplow blades raised up some inches above the road surface, so that only the fresh-fallen snow would get plowed to the sides of the streets, resulting in a good, hard-packed base on the streets. The banks along the streets rose up higher and higher through the winters, until it seemed to kids walking along that they were in a tunnel. When the steepest street in camp, White Avenue, became too icy for safety it was closed to traffic, because cars could not gain purchase and the plow crew used Thorpe Avenue to get to the higher streets. Climax's recorded snow fall from September to April, 1955-1956, was 242 inches! TWENTY FEET! And this wasn't even a record-setting winter.—

Once we arrive at the skating rink, it looks like at least fifty kids have got there ahead of us. We go right into the warm-up building, exchange snow boots for skates, and hurry right back outside. But no one is on the ice, yet.

"Hey, Deb! What're you doing?" Bobbie greets me, and jumps on my back, knocking me to my knees. She loves roughhousing, any chance she gets.

"Hi, Bobbie." I giggle as we roll around on the snowy ground. "Hey, how come no one's skating?"

"You goof! Don't you see Mr. DeMille out there?" she says, pointing to the far end of the rink.

"Oh, yeah." And sure enough, Blake DeMille is going back and forth, back and forth with a scoop shovel, clearing the ice of snow. And, although he moves quickly enough, it seems like eternity to us before we can start skating. We spend the waiting time sitting up on the concrete walls that surround the rink, horsing around and saying hi to all our friends. Bobbie and I greet dozens of kids from our class; after a while, Rosemary comes along with Sharon Shriver, whom I also happen to be good friends with.

Finally, Mr. DeMille signals that it's okay to get on the ice. We play "Crack the Whip" for a long time, then we have speed races, and we keep skating clear through lunchtime without realizing the number of hours that have passed by. Finally I begin to feel like my stomach is empty of everything but skin and bones, and since there are no snacks supplied in the warm-up building, we finally trudge back up the steep streets to our houses, compelled by hunger.

Dad shoveled the snow from our driveway all morning. He keeps a path cleared from the front door and the front walk that meets up with the driveway, because if the snow drifts against the garage door during the night, he can't push it open from the inside the next morning. For the first several snows he lifts the shovel and tosses the load to each side of the drive, but inevitably, the banks get extremely high, and it's unmanageable to heft the shovel way above his head, so he scoops the snow to the end of the driveway, and then the plows come by and push it to the street edges.

During blizzards, snow packs up against the house and within a few months, the snow piles up so high in places that it's only six inches or so to the rooftop. Many of the houses are flattops, which become one more fun playground for the kids. However, when the snow is that deep, it covers the house windows, which makes the inside rooms darkish, not enough for lights to be turned on, but almost.

Later on that same afternoon, we are outside playing, and the sky is still an exaggerated blue. I am bundled in a complete change of outdoor clothes, because my others got soaked at the skating rink. The three of us have two sets of everything, parkas, mittens, and snow pants. When we come in from outdoors freezing wet, Mom tosses everything into the dryer and by the time we've soaked the second set, the first set is ready to put back on, a practical system that assures we won't need to waste time waiting around, and we can return to our outdoor games quick-as-a-wink. Of course, this means the clothes dryer in our house runs continually.

Outside, Artie climbs up on the roof from the snow bank at the back of our house, which demands only modest effort. I trail him up there, and we jump off and climb back up, jump off and climb back up, time after time. After awhile, Becky comes out and plays on the roof with us. When she flops down on the roof and makes a snow angel, my brother and I make some, too.

"Hey, you guys, I'm going to put my skis on and ski off the roof," Artie announces.

But I glimpse fast-moving clouds on the hogback, and notice that Mt. Bartlett has become completely obscured. And before I can blink, blink, blink, clouds are racing right over 10th Street.

"Look at the sky, you guys," I exclaim, pointing my mittened hand up at Ceresco Ridge.

We stand transfixed watching the sky change from sunny blue to stormy gray, as fast as a finger snap. And then, before we can slide on our behinds down the driveway snow bank, the wind sets to howling like wild things have been unleashed, and snow conceals the world, like a stage curtain at the end of a performance. We race into the house for warmth and supper.

After supper all three of us start whining and whimpering, because our eyes are hurting like crazy. After Mom examines us, she determines that we have sunburned them from the glare of the bright sun reflecting off the white snow. She douses our eyes with eye drops, and places cool washcloths over them as we prepare for bed. We recover soon enough.

One Saturday morning during TV cartoons, Artie says, "Jacky and Joe and me are going up to the tanks with the toboggan, and sled all the way down from there on the service road."

Well. Becky and I hadn't thought of this marvelous idea before, so we exchange a smile, punctuated with arched eyebrows.

"That's a pretty good idea. I think that Debbie and I might go with you guys."

One endearing quality about my sister is that she considers me her right-hand man and automatically includes me when she decides to do something amusing. Together we take the toboggan out of mothballs, so to speak, while Artie goes off to get his friends.

Up the steep incline behind our house in the direction of the service road we trudge, dragging that darned heavy old wooden toboggan. Naturally, the first person in line has the toughest job, not only because of the depth of the snow on the unplowed service road, but each time their foot goes into the drift it must then be dragged back out for the next step. Someone trades off with the leader every few minutes, and our progress is gradual and laborious. We haven't even climbed halfway up to the tanks before everyone is tuckered out, and breathing like steam engines.

"I'm taking off my parka," I murmur, barely audible.

"Oh, no. You better not, your sweat will freeze right up, and before you know it, you'll be covered with a sheet of ice, and feel like a frozen pillar," Becky firmly advises me.

Sometimes my sister has a tendency to act bossy; but since she's frequently right, I leave my sweltering parka on, because the last thing I want to turn into is an ice sculpture. I struggle to keep my feet in the footsteps of the kids ahead, but I'm beginning to lack enthusiasm for this particular venture. Navigating in deep snow is strenuous, no matter how many kids are making a trail.

Presently, every one of us is stretched out on the vast snow mattress. We stuff handfuls of pristine snow into our mouths to relieve our dry throats of a thirst so fierce we're unable to swallow down spit.

Joe, leaning on his bent arms, sits up and suggests, "Let's just go up as far as that clump of trees." He takes off a mitten and points up the sloped road to a site that none of us can quite make out.

"Where, Joe?" Jacky asks, rolling from his back to his stomach.

"Those trees up there, see? Three, all together in a row?"

"Oh, yeah." We notice them now, and agree to go that much farther.

Once we reach the predetermined point, we scramble and struggle to get situated on the toboggan, but soon we arrive at the obvious conclusion that we simply will not all fit on the sled at the same time.

"Since it was my idea, Joe and Jacky and me get to go first," Artie declares to his sisters.

"Go on, who cares? Just hurry back up here, okay?" Becky mumbles around a mouth full of snow. I don't protest either, as his reasoning seems sound enough.

We watch as the boys go flying down the road. They appear to straddle the path we made, so that the toboggan will go faster, but the pitch of the incline accelerates the sled regardless. Sheets of snow fan out on either side like angel wings, and crystals of laughter trail after them. They fall off, get back on, and go again. After they get down to the bottom, though, they start waving and hollering up to us about something.

"What? What? We can't hear you!" Both Becky and I cup our hands around our mouths to add volume to our words. Jumping up and down, we continue bellowing until we're hoarse.

In time, the boys simply leave the hill, dragging the toboggan with them. We just can't believe our eyes! We're struck dumb with shocked disbelief.

"What do those little brats think they're doing?" Becky asks, incredulous, arms akimbo.

"It looks like they're not climbing back up here so that we can take a turn," I whisper, blinking rapidly, and dropping to my knees.

"Why, those insufferable rats! I'm telling on Artie as soon as we get home," Becky fumes, her fury coming out in gasps.

So, instead of the thrill of flying, Becky and I have to walk all the way back down the hill, utterly enraged and filled with growing contempt.

Becky storms into the house with me fluttering right on her heels. "Mom! Where's that big baby, Arthur?" Becky shrieks.

"Mom, where are you?" I call out, bending to dislodge my snowy boots.

"What is all the yelling about, girls? I'm right here," Mom says, coming into the kitchen with her arms full of laundry.

"Arthur"--we always call our brother "Arthur" when we're upset like this by his shenanigans—"and his brainless friends left Debbie and me at the very top of the hill after they'd already taken their turn on the toboggan. And we didn't even get one single ride. We had to walk all the way back down!" Becky is so livid, she bangs her fist on the countertop as she talks.

"Well, they must have had a good reason for leaving you. We'll just ask him as soon as he comes home," Mom says quite reasonably, and begins to sort the clothes into piles next to the washer.

"Oh, no. They did not have a good reason. No, they did not," Becky insists.

"Watch your tone, young lady," Mom warns.

When Artie gets home a while later, he comes into our bedroom where I'm playing dress-up with some old long dresses we got from our grandma's attic on the farm. Beck is sprawled on her bed reading a magazine.

"Get out of this room, you big baby!" she snarls, rising menacingly.

"How come you're so mad at me?" he asks with big wide eyes, sticking to the doorway in case he needs to make a quick retreat.

"Because, you and your dumb friends left us at the top of the hill, and we didn't even get one single turn," I say slowly, getting into the mood of the moment.

"Yeah. And I said to get out of this room," Becky repeats, as she strides across the room, glowering at him.

"Me and Joe had to go to the bathroom real bad. We yelled up to you girls that we'd be right back. So how's come you're so mad at me?" he explains in a whiny voice.

"Well, get out of here, anyway," Becky says--she dislikes having to swallow provocations down in one quick gulp.

"Girls, come and set the table for supper, please," Mom says, just as we plunk ourselves down in front of the TV a few minutes later. But just then the phone rings, and Becky leaps to answer it. While she's on the phone I go in the kitchen to start setting the table. We're having spaghetti and meat sauce tonight, which I moderately tolerate, but not the green beans . . . gag.

"Mom. Marilyn Dickeson wants to know if I can go skiing with her tomorrow. Can I?" Becky wants to know.

"I guess so. You should check with your father, first, though," Mom answers her.

So during supper Becky asks Dad if she can go skiing. He says it's okay with him, "If your mother thinks it's okay."

They do this a lot. Check with your father. Check with your mother.

"Okay, thanks. I'm going to call Marilyn as soon as we finish supper."

--People in Climax began skiing way back in 1937 when some Climax men got permission to build a small ski area on the east side of Chalk Mountain, just across the highway from the town. There was no ski lift, so people climbed to the top and then skied down. Climax skiers established the Continental Ski Club in 1941; after this, members were able to get the Company to help install a 1,800-foot rope tow and lights for night skiing. By the early '50s a T-Bar ski lift had been installed, new ski jumps made, and a two-story warm-up lodge with a ski shop had been built.

Families of Climax employees skied all year with a $10 season pass, and Max Schott School students could take skiing lessons on Tuesday and Thursday afternoons for fifty cents. My sister started skiing when she was just four years old. The Climax Ski Area was very popular, so much so, in fact, that during the first six days of the 1956 ski season 1,500 people had skied on the mountain.—

Sometimes Becky's a lucky duck, because she's the oldest, so she gets to do everything, before the idea even occurs to Artie or me. And, naturally, Artie's a lucky duck, because he's a boy. But just before we have to start getting ready for bed, and Mom has already put my hair up in curlers, the telephone rings, and it's for me! I become fairly charged with excitement, because I hardly ever receive phone calls.

"Mom, it's Rosemary on the telephone, and she wants to know if I can go skiing with her and her family tomorrow. Can I please?" I use my most sincere begging voice.

"We'll see, DoGo."

"But, Mom, she's on the phone right now, waiting for an answer."

"Oh, all righty. But be sure to let her know that you've only been skiing a few times, okay?" She didn't say to check with my father, because he's down at the Rec Hall with his bowling league tonight.

"Oh, goody!"

The following morning right after church, Becky and I get dressed in our warm ski clothes. Rosemary's dad picks me up and it looks to me like their station wagon is crammed with kids. Anyway, I squeeze into the back seat next to Rosemary and Caroline, her little sister. The little brothers are carrying on, because they're told to sit in the very back with all the skis and stuff.

After a good deal of time is wasted with minor preliminaries, my friend and I finally glide over to the ski-lift line.

"Let's get off at the fourth tower, okay, Rosemary?"

"Why? Don't you want to ski down all the way from the top of the mountain?"

"Well, this is just my fourth time skiing, and I only went up to the third tower those other times." Once on the lift I gaze all around at the evergreen trees covered with fresh snow, and then I glance up ahead at the steep, steep white-powdered slopes.

"Okay. We'll get off at the fourth tower," Rosemary agrees, and we hold each other's mittened hands as the T-bar lift sweeps us up the mountainside.

I am skiing with confidence, and we laugh exuberantly, rocketing through the bracing wind. After three successive runs, we elect to stop for a hot chocolate in the warming hut.

"Are you ready to go all the way to the top, yet, Debbie?" Rosemary asks, but she has whipped cream on the tip of her nose, which sends me into gales of laughter. She is good-natured, but only to a point. In time, she becomes exasperated with my silliness, so, by way of appeasement, I declare, "Yes, I'll go all the way to the top when we go back out."

Well, I am petrified as we ski off the lift at the top of Chalk Mountain; butterflies wreak havoc with my innards. Pausing on the pinnacle, we squint our eyes into slits and scrutinize the Climax camp for a minute or two.

"Can you make out your house? Let's see now . . ." Judging from minute square specks outlining the farthest perimeter of the town, I count, "One, two, there's my house, see, Rosemary?"

"Yep. I can see mine, too--way over there." And she points, her upper body bent frontward over her skis. "Okay, let's go."

I nod, and we're off, skimming down the mountain. We ski through deep powder as we maneuver through a stand of conifers, and my lissome heart floods with song. "Hot diggity, dog diggity, boom what you do to me!"

I trail Rosemary, but keep her red parka well within my range of vision, and before I know what's happening, we've skied to the upper edge of The Bowl! I struggle to catch my breath, as I snowplow to a standstill. I'm awash in trepidation, peering across this perilous basin.

--There exists a vast cirque, a natural steep-walled basin shaped like half a bowl, a quarter of the way down from the top of Chalk Mountain; the local skiers call it "The Bowl. It was a challenging run by any skier's standards. The young Climax men who went on to national skiing fame used this cirque to train for their competitions. This area turned out one Olympian, Dave Gorsuch, who represented the U.S. at Squaw Mountain, CA, in 1960. And two brothers, Scott and Rudd Pyles, competed on a national level during the '60s. I have skied at many resorts in Colorado as an adult--Vail, Aspen, and Steamboat, for instance, and in Utah at Snowbird and Alta--so I can claim with a good bit of authority that The Bowl at Climax was absolutely strenuous, an "expert" class ski run.—

"Jeepers, Rosemary! That slope looks beastly unmanageable from here." My voice shakes and my knees threaten to buckle under me. "Can't we just climb back up, and choose a different way down?" I implore my friend.

"My dad doesn't want me to ski over here, but if we just go as slow as we can, we'll be okay. Anyway, it will be easier than hiking back up the way we came, I think."

Slow is not a choice at all. Fast or faster is all we can muster. I drop to my behind every few feet or so, leaving a virtual wake of sitzmarks, as does Rosemary. And even after such an ungraceful display while descending the incline, I make it worse by plummeting in a somersault, tumbling in the fluffy powder the last dozen feet, and lose one of my skis because they lack safety straps.

Rosemary skis over to me and asks with dismay, "Debbie, did you hurt yourself?"

"No, but my ski went hurtling down the hill," I cry, shaking snow from inside my mittens, and otherwise setting myself to rights.

"Oh. Well, let's try skiing on three skis," she suggests.

And so, like a couple of clowns auditioning for what might be called "Ski Follies Unlimited," we hazard our way to the bottom of the hill, with me trying to keep my foot balanced on the back of her ski. This makes for a lot of mirth and merrymaking, to say nothing of the time it takes. But eventually we reach the bottom, and a Ski Patrolman is watching for me by the lodge, errant ski in hand.

"Is this yours, young lady?" he asks, solicitously.

"Uh-huh," I admit, nodding with embarrassment. Who else could it belong to?

"Well, you be sure to get some safety straps attached before you come over here again; an airborne ski turns into a javelin, and could cause serious injury."

"Yes, I'll tell my mom as soon as I get home," I promise the obliging patrolman.

On the way home Rosemary pipes up, "Dad, you should have seen how we had to ski down when Debbie lost her ski. It was the most fun we've ever had!"

--Some years after this, when I was eleven, Mom and Dad did purchase new ski equipment for me and Art and Becky. They bought the equipment at the Fremont Trading Post. My dear parents were not skiers, so they had to rely on some well-meant advice from a salesclerk. The skis they bought were functional, but the boots . . . The clerk told them that if we kids planned to use the boots for several years, then it would be wise to purchase a size 10 for each of us, as our feet would grow into them, and if we wore them with heavy socks, the boots would serve us quite well in the meantime. Well, neither Becky nor I ever wore a shoe size larger than a six. Nevertheless, we used the size 10 boots for five ski seasons. Was it no wonder then that our skiing technique flat-lined for years, because our feet slid to and fro inside the boots, as we attempted Christy turns on the slopes? And, apart from the difficulties on the slopes at Cooper Hill, Leadville's neighborhood ski area, we were exposed to streams of teasing and ridicule from friends who would quip, "Here come the Vincent sisters, skiing into the lodge on their boots again."

Early in 1942, the Army Corps of Engineers established Camp Hale, where the highly trained Tenth Mountain Division ski troopers were based. This army unit built the T-bar ski tow at Cooper Hill, and remained a presence at the ski area well into the '60s, helping the local Ski Patrol, and manning the ambulance when there were injuries. Becky had an accident once when a weighty T-bar bashed her in the back of the neck; the Camp Hale Ski Patrol took the utmost care in transporting her to Leadville's St. Vincent Hospital in an army ambulance.

Additionally of note, during WWII, the Climax Molybdenum Company warned the Camp Hale ski troopers not to Nordic-ski within Climax boundaries, as the specially trained guards were ordered to shoot at trespassers. And also, during these war years, those who skied at the

Climax Ski Hill were sternly cautioned not to ski out of bounds, because of the very real danger of Company attack dogs and armed guards.—

# Chapter Twelve

*All around the town people are talking about one thing. They collect in small knots of two or three, exchanging tidbits about halls decked with holly bows and sugar plum fairies dancing all over the place. Now and again, the little girl stands still, and listens to the talk. One group mentions a swaddled newborn baby and desert animals in a far-off land. The child smiles when she hears them talk, thinking that she'd like to visit such a place some day.*

--The Climax camp was truly beautiful during the holiday season, because the Electrical Department spent days stringing lights and decorations. Santa and his reindeer sat atop the guard house to greet people, the radio tower by the gate was strung with lights in the shape of a giant tree, the #3 mill building which faced Highway 91 had a colossal star on its facade, and many Company buildings, including the Rec Hall and the black water tower, were draped with hundreds of lights. Indeed, this dazzling splendor propelled the community into an exuberant holiday spirit.—

Soon school will be out for two weeks because it's Christmas vacation. On the last day, my class has a fun-filled Christmas party, and my mom is there as a room mother to help Mrs. Ross. I'm very contented because Francis Gill got moved into Mrs. Dryden's class three weeks ago, because our class had too many kids, so now I don't have to be on the lookout for idiotic notes left clandestinely on my desktop! Marilyn Distler and Sherry Phelps got moved, too, and they are my friends, but we still get to play together at recess. When I do see Francis at a safe distance in the hallway, I try to smile a tiny bit at him, because of my mom's suggestion.

Mom baked chocolate cupcakes yesterday for my class's party, and we have a teensy tiny blue spruce to decorate, later. Any time that we have parties, kids may sit wherever they want, so I ask Gary Ohmert to trade desks with me, and he does, and now, Bobbie and I are next to each other, which means that we can horse around and giggle about stuff.

"Hey, Debbie, what did you get Mrs. Ross for a present?" Bobbie asks, licking pink frosting from a cupcake, while taking care to save the candy snowman for last.

"Oh, some nice handkerchiefs. What did you?" I'm meticulously unwrapping a candy cane as I watch Jimmy Ducharme and Larry Joe Burgess play a version of rock, paper, scissors, each trying to win the extra cupcake; I'm hoping that Larry Joe wins.

"My mom made me wrap up some hose to give her," she says, with knitted brow.

"What? A hose? That is a peculiar present--what would Mrs. Ross want a hose for?" I wonder, as giggles begin to bubble up, because an image of our teacher lugging a coiled green water hose around with her materializes in my mind.

"Not that kind of hose, you goof! Hose to wear on your legs," Bobbie says, still looking troubled.

"You gave the teacher underwear? Jeepers!"

I am flooded with sympathy for my friend, because I know Mrs. Ross will most likely hold the underwear up high, so that everyone can see. That's the way teachers usually do. Mrs. Ross has an impressive pile of presents on her desk now, and all of us get to cluster around so that we can see her reactions. She's having a high old time, and sure enough she holds each kid's gift up so everyone can goggle at it; inevitably, when she opens Bobbie's, three dimwitted boys standing nearby snort and snicker. I command them to shush up in a loud whisper. Poor Bobbie's face has switched from normal to a sickly, mottled scarlet.

"Don't pay any attention to those idiotic boys, Bobbie," I advise, attempting to comfort her. It helps that Mrs. Ross behaves as if she likes getting hose for a present, so everything is okay.

When it's time, we go over by the tree with offerings of scratched glass balls and crumply tinsel from our homes, and then take turns hanging our decorations. Each of us has made a sparkly bell or star during art time all week, so we hang these on the tree, too, then we stand back to admire our handiwork. Personally, I'm touched by its homeliness, and am determined to love it, the same as I would a scraggly mongrel that might think me its master.

For the last hour of the afternoon, we troop over to the gym for our Christmas Program. Dad has taken time off from his job to be here. All of the school kids sit in the bleachers until it's time for each individual class to sing, then we clamber onto the gym floor in turn, and perform rehearsed, holiday songs under the basketball net. When it comes time for my class to present our part we scramble from the bleachers, but I stumble, falling to my knees and skinning my shin, which makes it very difficult for me to sing "We Wish You A Merry Christmas" with tears in my throat, but I somehow manage.

Today is the Saturday that Mom and Dad are going to an elegant Company dinner/dance affair down at the Rec Hall. It's an especially blustery morning, snowing and blowing to beat the band, so we don't play outside very long. No matter, we're quite keyed up and excited at the prospect of having a babysitter tonight. The daylight hours slog sluggishly along, and I eventually fall asleep in the afternoon, which is astonishing, because I haven't taken naps since kindergarten.

Mom and Dad are all dressed up for their party. Dad looks like a dignified TV announcer wearing a dark suit, and he's chosen to wear his burgundy tie with a design of miniature silver reindeer that we gave him for Christmas last year. I think he looks especially elegant, and the perfect escort for Mom in her trendy creation, a knee-length melon-colored satin sheath with a stiff, netted overskirt. Her earrings are dangly sparkles and her sling-back high heels match her cocktail bag. But Mom puts on snow boots for now, and stashes her dress-up shoes in a bag to wear when she gets to the Rec Hall.

And then, at long last, our babysitter arrives. We kiss Mom and Dad goodbye, while they both keep directing us to behave ourselves with the sitter. I think they're concerned that we might be plotting some kind of shenanigans, or something, but we're really and truly not.

Ellen Butler is an attractive, perky high school girl, and we feel privileged that she has agreed to watch us. She's special, because for one thing, her boyfriend is on the Blue Devils basketball team playing a game down in Salida, which is why she doesn't have anything else to do tonight except look after us. She also just happens to be a popular Blue Devils cheerleader, but the cheering squad doesn't always go to the out-of-town games. She wears her cropped brown hair in soft curls around her face, and she looks very hip dressed in blue jeans with bobby sox and loafers. For me, it's her velvety soft voice along with her sunny smile that lights up a room that floods my heart with fond feelings.

--The Max Schott Blue Devils was a winning basketball club, and the *Moly Mountain News* was regularly filled with statistics touting their successful seasons. At the end of the '53-'54 season—as well as the previous year--they had advanced to the Division A State Championship; that season the players included Richard Anderson, Waldo Gordon, Bill Cerise, George Arnold, Jim Phillips, and Richard Cunningham. Gilbert Boyd, Eugene O'Barr, Carl Arnold, Bill Killinen, Chuck Harnish, Bill Gregory, Fred Mondragon, Lloyd Morris, Bob Walker, and George Young played for the Blue Devils during the '56-'57 basketball season. The young men were heroes in the eyes of the Climax citizens, and several hundred fans packed the school gym whenever they had a game. My folks attended these, as well as many of the out-of-town tournaments, to cheer the Blue Devils on to victory.—

This evening, in an attempt to win Ellen's undying allegiance, Beck, Art and I vow to remain on our best behavior, so we begin by offering our help in getting supper ready. Earlier in the day, Becky had said to me that if Ellen liked us, it would be to our credit, and we'd more than likely reap countless rewards. When I asked her what kind of rewards, she just gave me one of her know-it-all looks. So . . .

"I know where Mom stores the glasses, Ellen," I say, pulling myself up on the countertop, so that I can stretch to the highest shelf in the cupboard. She watches as I grasp in my hand two exquisite cordial glasses with fragile stems that are rarely used, most definitely never by us, and then I delicately transfer them into Becky's waiting hands.

"I don't think those should be used; the way they're stored probably means that they're quite cherished," Ellen says, but then she has to quickly turn her attention back to the meat sizzling in a skillet on the stove.

"Oh, yeah, we are supposed to," Becky insists, placing the glasses around the table. "Mom says we should use these whenever we want, not just for special occasions. As a matter of fact, she likes us to use them, so that they won't collect dust in the cupboard."

"Hmmm. Well, everyone sit down now, so we can eat before it gets cold."

Along with the chopped veal cutlets--one of our favorites, because of the savory crispness along the edges--she also serves green beans.

I tell Ellen, grimacing with revulsion at my plate, "I am allergic to green beans; they always make me throw up whenever I'm forced to eat them."

"You little liar! You do not throw up, you just don't ever like eating any kind of vegetables; but you have to anyway," Becky says, with an especially high-and-mighty attitude.

"Well, don't talk about that now, or everyone will lose their appetites," Ellen says, holding her fork suspended in midair above her plate, looking deliberately into our eyes.

"Okay," I agree, while bestowing upon Ellen my most enchanting smile, because I really want more than anything for her to like me, so that she'll want to come back and sit for us in the future.

"You forgot to give us something to drink, Ellen," Artie says, holding his flimsy, petite glass out to her.

"Oops. I did forget. Just a second." She goes to the Fridge for a carton of milk, pours it for us, and then sets the carton on the table; but the three of us must reach for it again and again refilling the miniscule glasses.

Inevitably, disaster happens when Artie loses his grip on the carton, and milk splashes everywhere like a tidal wave, soaking everything in sight, and naturally, his tiny little glass shatters on the floor, as he leaps in alarm from his chair.

"Uh-oh, now you're really in for it! You broke one of Mom's best glasses!" Becky laments.

Artie starts to wail wretchedly, which makes me snivel sympathetically, because about three different times throughout the meal my own delicate glass almost slipped from my hand.

Ellen fumes and storms about the kitchen, her face a heightened color, and she is entirely livid about having been duped into using the special glasses, so now she shoos us into the living room while she restores order to the kitchen without having us underfoot.

Becky turns on the TV, but there's nothing on for us to watch, just news programs about President Eisenhower and politics. Boring.

"Hey, Beck, would you read us a story from the *Dickens Stories about Children* book?" I ask because I enjoy the way she reads, with flair, never skipping over the difficult words.

"Okay." She turns off the television set, and lifts a hardbound volume from the bookcase where all the valued books are shelved. My brother and I settle on the couch; he has only just now recovered his composure from the spilt-milk fiasco. Whoever spoke the old adage, "Why cry over spilt milk?" would have swallowed his words back down, if he'd been in our house tonight, I'm thinking.

"I'm going to read this story called 'The Fat Boy,'" she decides, just as Ellen enters the room. She seems tranquil now; not a sign of her former fury remains.

"What are you kids doing?" she asks.

"Reading from the Charles Dickens collection. Um, Ellen, would you read it to us?" Becky asks, with an ingratiating smile.

"Okay. Sure. Is this the one you want, 'The Fat Boy'?" she wants to know, looking at the book, as she sits on the couch between Artie and me.

"Yep." Eager to dispel any lingering annoyance she might have regarding our behavior, we agree.

Pretty Ellen begins to read the story; it's a story that makes us sad, and even though we've listened to it before, Artie and I get choked up in the parts when people boss Joe, the poor fat boy, around, and insist that he do all the rough work.

"Thanks, Ellen, for reading to us. Now can we make some fudge?" Becky asks.

I lift my eyebrows in awe at my sister's self-assured manner.

"Okay, but your mom might not have all the ingredients on hand. Let's go look."

I think, *Wow! Having a sitter is so fantastic! Especially when mine is willing to do almost anything she's asked.*

Ellen takes a considerable amount of time locating the necessary items, but finally she manages. She combines everything in the pan on the stove, and then we help her by taking turns stirring the mixture, and stirring, and stirring. But nothing happens--the concoction stays runny like slushy spring water. Finally, Artie asks if we can just go ahead and eat the fudge with spoons, and Ellen agrees to let us do this. It tastes sugary-sweet like it's supposed to, but it really is just icing, not fudge.

And then it is time for prayers and bed. Ellen listens to us say our prayers and this is nice, because we have been saying our prayers silently for a long time, not out loud, so as I recite them now I fancy that I'm sharing God with her. And this idea makes me hug Ellen and I kiss her pink powdered cheek. I love our babysitter!

Sometime within the week, my whole family is invited to the Shrivers' Christmas party. At their house we play with Sharon, who's in my class, and Billy, who's the same age, but in Mrs. Dryden's. Sharon, Billy, and the oldest boy Bill, who's in high school, are not true sister and brothers, but Dad once explained that Bill and Sharon's mom died in a tragic fire in a trailer down by Grand Junction where they had a fruit orchard. And after a considerable amount of time had passed, her dad, Warren, married Billy's mom, Marge, making them stepchildren. Anyway, we play board games for hours in the back bedrooms, and eventually, the Shrivers' house becomes choked with cigarette smoke and the clamor of revelers.

Spread out on a table in the living room are canapés and cold cuts and fancy dessert fantasies, so we gobble snacks like ducks gorging on breadcrumbs at a park. After a considerably long time, Artie and I start sipping from glasses that people keep on setting down on the table, and then they walk off chatting, forgetting to come back for their drinks. Shortly, both of us get kind of woozy and wobbly, and the next thing I know it's the following morning, and I'm in the bathroom with my head in the toilet throwing up again and again, and Artie takes turns doing the same.

I overhear Mom and Dad exclaim that we are both drunk! Now how did that happen? My little brother and I are sick in bed for the entire long day. Jeepers!

Christmas inches stealthily into sight, so my family decorates the six-foot blue spruce tree that stands regally in front of the living room windows. After we have garishly laden it with lights and colored bulbs and tinsel, we spend hours wrapping presents with holiday paper and ribbons. Mom makes popcorn and offers eggnog with nutmeg before it's time for bed; we are happily satiated with holiday treats and traditions.

In the wee hours of the night, Becky and I are startled from our sleep by a thunderous crash!

"What was *that?*" I ask, rubbing my sleepy eyes.

"I have no idea. Let's go see," she cries out, and we scurry down the hall to the living room.

Mom and Dad stand together, staring forlornly at our beautiful Christmas tree lying in a disastrous heap on the floor.

"What happened to the tree?" Becky asks, when she's able to utter a sound.

"Your father will explain," Mom intones, unhappy and somehow disconnected with the surreal image.

"I stuck the tree trunk into a bucket of sand that I had out in the garage to hold the tree upright and stable," he says to us, rubbing his rumpled forehead. "But the sand must have frozen up around the darned thing when I left it out there overnight. Anyway, the sand melting inside the container caused the tree to topple over. Now, you people go on back to bed so your mother and I can get this mess cleaned up. Goodnight."

"Goodnight," my sister and I mumble at the same time.

Just as I'm nodding off for the second time, Becky whispers that she can hear reindeer paws on our roof. I concentrate very hard, but cannot hear a solitary sound--the night is hushed and empty as a snow cave. I keep on trying for some time, but my eyelids have heavy weights dragging on them, so I fall into a deep sleep.

Naturally, we wake up at the very crack of dawn, but tiptoeing from the bedroom I'm sluggish, and struggle to dispel foreboding visions of what we might be faced with in the living room. But Mom and Dad have accomplished a miracle fixing everything up, because it just looks the same as it did, except with fewer lights and bulbs on the branches, but okay just the same.

My family always has Christmas after Santa Claus has been to our house at daybreak, just as the sun begins to dance on the tips of the surrounding peaks. We are very excited about the surprises under the tree: Becky receives a nursing research kit; Artie, an archery set; and I get the drum majorette outfit that I requested in my Santa letter. Surrounded by my family, a magical and tender moment embraces and captivates me.

A couple of nights after Christmas, Dad toils in the kitchen creating heaps of little meat and cheese sandwiches and crackers stacked with cheese and olives, and he dumps bags of potato chips into bowls and prepares dips, because some adult friends are coming to our house for a holiday party. Our Fridge is stocked with soda cans and on the counter an arrangement of liquor bottles await the arrival of guests.

Artie's eyebrows lift as he whispers, "I know one thing's for sure--I'm not drinking from anybody's glass this time, are you, Debbie?"

Pausing to inspect the array of bottles, I grasp hold of his hand, and murmur, "Don't remind me about that stupid time. I don't even want to think about it ever again." And then, peering into the depths of his wide, brown eyes I add, "I hope that I'll never, as long as I live, ever feel as sick as a dog, like we both did that time."

Meanwhile, dozens of festively adorned grownups begin amassing in our living room. Then, dressed in our pajamas, we file through the room to politely say "Hello" to our parents' friends. Our ardent vows regarding booze are pointless and superfluous, as we say a hasty goodnight, kiss Mom and Dad on the cheek, and then hustle off to bed.

A bit later, snuggled in bed, Becky whispers to me, "The Priers said that they heard reindeer paws on their roof Christmas Eve, just like I did. Are you absolutely positive that you didn't hear any reindeer paws, Debbie?"

Unaware that she is goading me, I say naively, "Yes, I'm completely sure. Even though every inch of me was busting with wishing for it, I just couldn't stay awake waiting and listening." And then I have to swallow hard and blink rapidly to hold my tears at bay, knowing I must somehow be unworthy to hear the magic of the reindeer paws, and worse than this, now it seems that I'm the only one who did not get to hear them. Some sympathetic star must be sticking close to my sister, and that's why she's so darned lucky.

On New Year's Eve, we're given another opportunity to have Ellen Butler sit with us, again. Well, elated and exuberant, we anticipate an evening of merriment. It's hard for us to hold our over-stimulation in check while waiting for her to come. The three of us boisterously roughhouse like frenzied chimpanzees on a rampage, jumping and running around all over the house.

"You people settle down before I have to warm your behinds!" Dad warns us, entering the living room and flipping on the television set.

We make an earnest attempt to settle down, because, for sure, I don't want my behind all warmed up. Then, to pass the time, my sister and I saunter into Mom's bedroom and watch her getting ready.

"Are you wearing the melon dress tonight?" I ask, as she finishes polishing her nails a bright scarlet color. Beck and I are lolling on top of the big bed, and I trace a gold leaf in the bedspread pattern with my finger.

"No, DoGo. I'm wearing the black velvet outfit hanging on the closet door."

--I wore this very same evening outfit of Mom's--black velvet Capri pants and a fitted top with a deeply cut V in back and three quarter sleeves--on New Year's Eve twenty years later. Although Mom had taken great pains over the years to keep it in mint condition, at the end of the evening, while getting into the car, the entire inner leg seem ripped from stem to stern--the fit had been perfect, but the fabric was rotten with age.—

"That will look smashing, Mom," Becky compliments her, and I heartily agree, gushing, "Mom, you will be the most elegant lady at the party," just as Artie calls out, "Ellen's here, you guys."

We rush headlong into the living room and parrot, "Hi, Ellen!"

"Hello." Tonight she's wearing her blue jeans with a bulky pink cable-knit cardigan. And she's brushed her hair into a very short ponytail, tied with a filmy blue scarf.

Mom and Dad both tell us with undue excess to behave ourselves before they leave. Personally, I feel they're giving Ellen the unfair impression that we're lacking in trustworthiness and self-control.

"What should we do tonight, Ellen?" Becky asks for the three of us. Lots of times Becky does the talking for us by virtue of seniority and sophistication.

"I want to watch Guy Lombardo on TV. He's doing a special program for New Year's Eve," she says, while hanging her coat in the hall closet.

Well, this doesn't sound like very much fun to us, but nevertheless, we position ourselves on the couch with her and watch for an interminable number of minutes.

"Want to make fudge again, Ellen?" Becky asks, fiddling with Artie's toy dump truck on the arm of the couch.

"No thanks. You kids can go play in your rooms for a while, okay?" She smiles, but doesn't take her eyes from the TV.

"Humph." Becky marches off down the hall with Artie and me right on her heels into us girls' bedroom.

"How do you like that?" Becky asks with dramatic flair. My sister can sure work herself up into a lather when situations don't go in the precise direction she thinks they should go. I happen to have plenty of first-hand experience with this particular side of her personality.

"I don't like it," Artie says, but he's already jumping from Becky's bed to mine in his Superman outfit, so his opinion is disregarded as lacking in sincerity.

"Me either," I agree adamantly. But then, being unsure about the rules when it comes to babysitters, I ask, "Is Ellen required to play with us all the time, Becky?"

"Yes, she most certainly is. And I'm telling on her just as soon as Mom gets home, too."

*Well now. This puts a whole different light on the matter,* I silently reflect.

"Come on, you guys. Let's go in the kitchen and make ice cream floats," Beck urges us; and with a particularly bold display of dissension, she tromps down the hall, again with me and Artie trailing in the lower ranks. We don't speak a single word to Ellen on our way through the living room to the kitchen.

Becky hauls down some glasses from the cupboard, and barks, "Debbie, get the carton of ice cream out of the freezer. And, Artie, you get the root beer bottle and put it on the table."

My brother and I snap to attention, following orders without any fuss.

We pour root beer into the glasses and Becky plunks ice cream in on top. But the concoction continues bubbling and foaming all over the table like emerging lava from a volcano, which sends us into hysterical laughter, as we cannot hold back the overflowing mess.

Eventually Ellen comes in to see what we're up to and asks what's going on. Her eyes sweep over the mess, and with arms akimbo, she demands, "Who gave you kids permission to make ice cream floats?"

"My mom said we could before she left," Becky states, using her most self-assured tone.

"Well, your mom said nothing to me, and I think she would have, don't you? Now, clean up the mess you've made before you even think about leaving this kitchen." And, turning on her heel, she walks out.

Becky mutters that we better mind Ellen, or we might get into trouble when Mom and Dad get home from their party, so we do clean up. But first we slurp as much of the messy treat as possible from the glasses, and in so doing, get a modicum of satisfaction from our rebellious activity.

At last, we shift into the living room; Ellen's program is still on TV, so we sit on the couch and take a second crack at watching it with her.

"Hey, Ellen, I'm going to stay up all night until it's the new year," I declare, just to see if I can get a reaction from her. But she does not swallow the bait. Instead, she shrugs her shoulders and says, "Okay."

*Ah ha!* For a while I brood over her lack of concern. Eventually, out of a feeling of frustration, I initiate some strife with Artie by punching his arm. And of course he punches me back, but before the situation can escalate, Ellen fastens a glowering frown on us and pointedly clears her throat. He and I immediately get the picture and settle down, but this hiatus is short-lived.

Eventually, Artie and I get so bored with Ellen's program, before you know it, we're dive-bombing from the back of the couch onto the stuffed chair, playing Superman.

"Stop the roughhousing, you kids," Ellen says about a jillion times.

We're having such a howling good time--now immersed in contesting who can execute the longest jump--it's nearly impossible to end our sport.

"If you don't stop the jumping, I'm going to give you a swat!" Ellen warns us one final time, and raises herself from the couch, smoothing her hair back into the ponytail.

Well, this registers to me as a double-dare, and I doubt seriously that she has the nerve to smack us, so I glance at Artie and he gets my meaning: "Let's just keep on horsing around and jumping from the furniture, 'cause we're having too much fun."

And before I know what's happening, Ellen smacks me soundly on the behind!

"Ouch! That hurts!" I yelp, indignantly.

"I warned you over and over again. Now, go to your rooms and get your pajamas on! And then you can both just get into bed!"

Since Becky has played no part in our capers, she's privileged to stay up for a while longer.

And I am utterly distressed, because, although I'm unsure, I wonder whether or not Ellen gave my brother a swat. I'm fairly certain that *I'm* the only one she swatted. But I don't ponder this point for long, because alone in the quiet darkness of my bedroom a sinking sensation settles over me: Oh, boy! This is a dire misfortune. My brother and I will probably be in heaps of trouble with Mom and Dad when they hear the report, and then we'll be punished. And at length, with all this agony and regret churning in my head, I surrender to sleep; but first, I fervently say my prayers.

In the end, Ellen does not tattle, but instead elects to keep her own council, illustrating why she remains in my heart the most superior babysitter of all time. And, in fact, the next time she comes over to our house I will dazzle her with my sterling character and exemplary manners.

# Chapter Thirteen

*There are some storms that in their ferocity, can obliterate a landscape, destroy every landmark of human civilization, and wreak such immense havoc, as to bring an entire community to its knees. What then of the storm, that in its intense fury, transforms the inner spirit of the child, once clenched in its relentless jaws, to such an extent that forever after leaves the youth unafraid to face down any peril?*

Climax skies turn mauve to peachy pink to creamy gray, and then darkness falls like a curtain in wintertime. When we get home from school it only remains daylight briefly, and then the world is obscured until the streetlights go on. Artie and I, and sometimes Becky, too, like to play outside in the snow before it's time for supper. We almost always play at jumping off the roof, and sometimes we drag the toboggan up there and try to slide down, but this doesn't work too well, mostly.

Today my brother and I are making snow angels in the soft, fresh fallen snow, like Becky showed us; it's snowing softly with no blowing wind, and giant flakes float down and melt on our upturned faces; as, with wide-open mouths, we manage to seize some on our hot tongues.

"Let's go over and see if the Ducharmes can play, okay?" Artie asks.

"Nah. You can, but I'm staying here. Jimmy and me are in a fight, because at school today he claimed that I don't know how to draw a map of Africa, when anyone bothering to study my drawing could see it was perfect."

I imagine that Jimmy must spend wakeful hours at night designing tactics about how he can next hurt my feelings. He's become first-rate at it, but I am determined not to squander my energy paying attention to his unbearable attitude, and I certainly will not play with him, right now.

"Okay. Let's build a snow fort, then," Artie suggests, because he's seemed to notice how often Jimmy plucks away at me, and his face floods with momentary sympathy.

"Okay! That's a good idea! I'll locate the shovel." Sliding rapidly from the towering bank, I land abruptly on my behind in the driveway, then into the garage I tramp.

The snow shovel is cumbersome and heavy for me to haul to the towering crest of the snow bank. This type has a square flat scoop that's likely made out of extra solid steel, with an unnecessary length of handle; in fact, if I measure it next to me the handle is a good three feet above my head. I'd bet that it would exist longer than the dinosaurs did during their reign, never wearing out or falling apart. It takes a while, but I heft it along to the pinnacle where Artie has been waiting, and now he stretches out to me, attempting to gain purchase of the unwieldy shovel for the final section, and relieves me of my burden. I smile my thanks at him.

We take turns plowing and bashing into the snow mount using the heaviest shovel in the entire lower forty-eight. After straining a while, we manage to hollow out a decent-sized cave, one affording room enough for two to squeeze tightly into together; and, once inside our snow cave quiet stillness envelops us. I shut my eyes and use only my ears to detect the universe, but there are no sounds; there is absolute silence.

"Listen, Artie. Not a solitary peep in the whole wide world."

"Yeah. I know. I can't hear any noises, either."

"Debbie and Artie! Time to come in for supper!" Becky bellows from the kitchen door in the garage.

"Coming!" We holler back at exactly the same time, and then we slide into the driveway carrying a whole ton of snow down with us. Both of us totally forget about the snow shovel that belongs in the garage.

After supper Dad gets his warm, bulky clothes on, and goes out to shovel snow from the driveway. He comes back in immediately, shouting at us. "Where in the Sam Hill is the snow shovel? You people get your coats on, and get out here right now and find it!"

"Uh-oh, Debbie. Remember we left it up on top of the snow bank?" Artie says, with big wide eyes.

"Oh, yeah. You and me left it up there just before supper. Who wants to go get it for Dad, me or you?" I ask, laying the charm on thickly.

"I'll go, I guess," he decides, generously, and I am very keen on my brother for performing this favor.

Later on, I perch on a chair at the kitchen table studying my spelling words, and Becky's laboring over her arithmetic homework. I'm quite fond of spelling, and I finish with my list in short order. Then, I find Mom in the living room stitching a tear in my brother's pants.

"Mom, I'm done with my spelling words. Do you want to see if I know them?"

"Yes." She smiles, and then gives me my words, which I'm able to spell easily.

When we get up for school in the morning, the wind is howling like banshees. We gobble cream of wheat and cinnamon toast, and I remain at the table ruminating over the snow bank that completely obliterates the view from the kitchen window, while Becky gets her school clothes on. I've already been dressed for an hour.

"Hey, where's Artie, anyway, Mom? He's going to make us late for school, if he doesn't hurry up," I lament, after realizing that I haven't seen a glimpse of my brother this morning.

"I'm keeping him home from school today. Your father and I were up all night with him, fighting his high fever. I'm sure that he's coming down with a nasty cold this morning."

"Oh. Is he still in bed?" I ask, concerned because we are hardly ever sick enough to have to stay in bed.

"Uh-huh. And let's just let him sleep, okay?" Mom is peering out the living room window, which seems to me an exercise in futility, since the snow is as high as the roof, just as it has been since about Thanksgiving-- how could she manage to forget that? Her behavior puzzles me. She sure seems worried about something.

"What's wrong, Mom? How come you're staring out the window when there's nothing to see?" I ask the back of her colorfully striped blouse.

"It's really dreadful out there, more so than I can ever remember seeing it. I don't think you girls should go to school in this storm," Mom says just as Becky walks into the room, fiddling with the belt of her dress.

"What? But we always go to school! Don't make us stay home today, please, Mom!" Becky stretches to her full height, and appears ready to take on a full army. "I have to go, I just have to."

"Please don't make us stay home like babies, Mom," I wail, parroting my sister's pleas. But, while not desiring whines to diffuse any strength of position, I keep my tone composed. "I must go to school, too, Mom."

"Oh, girls, all right. You can go to school, but I certainly do not think it's a very smart idea, at all." Her face is deeply swathed in worry as she speaks.

Becky and I drag on our snow pants, parkas, boots, mittens, and then Mom wraps a soft, woolen scarf around each of our faces.

"You girls stay on the road, okay? No shortcuts." She recites imperatives one after the other. "Do not get lost in the snow. Stay with each other, promise?" She stands at the kitchen door that opens out to the garage.

"Okay, we promise. Don't worry, Mom," Becky mumbles into the scarf that covers all but her eyes.

Becky and I tread down the drive and out onto 10th Street. The howling wind immediately knocks into us with a force, very much like that tractor tire of ours barreling downhill. As we set to walking on our street not far from our house, I comfort myself by thinking that this is nothing but an ordinary snowstorm, and anyway, we're used to being out in ghastly weather. And, actually, the snow and wind do ease up fractionally if we hug closely against the plowed snow bank that edges the road, because the bank lends a bit of protection, like a wall. I peer into the storm, figuring that we're near Rosemary's house, but everything around us is obscured from view by the storm.

As we round the corner of 10th and labor down to 9th Street, the snow and wind slam into us so powerfully that we nearly fall down. Becky grasps hold of my hand firmly, and sort of starts tugging me along. Each footstep is awkward for us, as the wind thunders dead-on into the front of us, blasting our faces and by now my woolen scarf has stiffened with my icy spit. The snow continues to dump down as thickly and heavily as can be conceived. We haven't seen a house, a car, or another living soul since our journey began, and, although it's downhill all the way from this point, we can barely move one foot in front of the other. A pair of snails could travel along faster than we can, but snails would freeze instantly on this brutal Arctic morning.

At length, we pass 8th Street, and obstinately force ourselves along curvy 5th Street, nearing the halfway point to the school. Both of us are breathing heavily, because we're tiring out fighting against the snow and wind pummeling us. I'm finding it a challenge just to move my lips. A powerful gust crashes into us with the force of an avalanche, knocking me backward to the frozen ground and tearing Becky's hand from my grip. Scared as I have ever been in my whole life, I shriek, "Don't lose me! Becky, please help me, I can't get up!"

But my words are snuffed out by the blasting gale and for the first time I have doubts that we can successfully combat the storm. I think about turning back. Keep going? Turn back? But, because now that we're as close to school as we are to home, turning back just doesn't seem sensible, somehow.

In no time, Becky struggles back to where I'm crouched into a ball on the road, heaves me onto my feet, and seizes hold of my arm. She yells out something, but the powerful storm snatches her words from me. We battle arduously into the relentless jaws of the demon force, each and every step a strenuous challenge to gain forward progress. And still, the ongoing, emotional, internal war continues in my head. Go on? Turn back? Go on? Turn back? While part of me knows that I must hold onto every ounce of courage to support my sister's efforts, the spit stuck to the back of my throat, and the frozen tears on my face worsen the situation even further, which simply advances the shriveling and shrinking of my steadfastness. Turn back?

Although we know that we holler in vain, Becky nevertheless tries every so often to shout something to me. Another extremely powerful gale of snow-laden wind again bashes into us, knocking us both to our knees, so we just hunker down and huddle with our arms tight around one another, struggling to catch our breath; breathing in and out seems nearly as demanding as the storm itself.

At length, we once more set out, hobbling slowly along, our bodies stooped like ancient invalids, until finally we must turn and walk backward against the wind, because our faces are painfully frozen, and worse than this, eyelashes iced with snow constrict our vision, further testing us, severely. We turn around and face forward again, because backward progress proves next to nothing. No matter, my sister perseveres onward, brazening out the misery of the intense storm, and, since I'm knocked down every step or two, she must battle for both of us.

At long last, we find ourselves at the corner of 4th Street; but I know this only because I see a "4"on the street sign that whips to and fro in the severe wind. Truly, the full concentrated power of the storm crushes down on us now, and bent double, I try with all my might to move, but I cannot inch forward even a fraction.

I am shuddering and trembling with cold and terror, and my head pounds with the ongoing roar of the storm's fury. I give up; I cannot fight the blizzard anymore. I stop.

Becky turns instantly and looks at me, and then she lumbers the two steps back to my side. Without hesitating, she zips her parka open, hugs me against her, and sets her back against the harsh, bashing wind blasts, while holding wide the bottom ends of her coat, so that the strength of the powerful wind won't succeed in slamming me to the ground. Agonizing slowly, with me protected by my sister, we struggle painfully onward, all the while being thrashed and battered about, until, miraculously, we manage to crawl together up the stairs of the school.

Two teachers, Mrs. Ross and Mrs. Monk, push against the force of the wind, making a great effort to get the school door open just enough for us to squeeze through.

"We've been standing here quite a while watching two little specks of color get bigger and nearer to the school. We really could not believe our eyes, when we finally realized that what we were seeing were two children," Mrs. Ross tells us, as she helps us to wriggle out of our frozen clothes.

"Neither one of us can quite believe how brave you little girls are. Imagine! Out there battling this blizzard, for all you're worth! I'll go to the office right away to see if I can get through to your mother on the phone," Mrs. Monk says, after she has us both settled next to her classroom's radiator.

For some long minutes, Mrs. Ross keeps on trying to rub some warmth back into our hands and feet. Our noses drip like leaky faucets, so she leaves the room to get us some tissues. She returns to where we sit next to the spitting radiator.

"Who else is at school today, Mrs. Ross?" Becky asks, after she's thawed out considerably.

"Well, dear, Mrs. Monk and I drove down here together first thing this morning, only to find that we were the only two teachers in the building. Some high school kids managed to drive here just a short time ago; we told them to turn around and go back home. I hope they haven't gotten their car stuck in a snow bank. We suggested that they use Thorpe Avenue, but we watched them as they turned out of the parking lot and drove off in the opposite direction. We were talking about that and studying the storm from the door's window when we noticed you two, and I have to say, admired your determination to get here as you got nearer and nearer. So, Becky, to answer your question, no one else but you two small children came to school today in this severe blizzard."

"Just me and my little sister," Becky states, and then, with her cocky, self-confident smile in place, she puts her arm around me.

--Mr. C.D. Snyder and the Max Schott School Board never once considered closing the school for a "snow day." In fact, the idea was entirely unheard of. After all, if they had done so, students would have ended up with an 80- or 90-day school calendar, rather than the regulation 180-day calendar year. I, personally, had never heard the term "snow day" until I began teaching in the Jefferson County school district, many years later.

Oh, and this 1956 blizzard dumped twenty-five inches of snow on Climax in six hours with winds gusting up to 85 miles an hour! These statistics were recorded at the High Altitude Observatory (the Harvard College Observatory) situated on the north slope of Chalk Mountain. There may have been worse storms before that one, and maybe even after, but Becky and I, together, battled and survived one very severe blizzard nevertheless.—

# Chapter Fourteen

*Bright yellow crocuses and tiny sprouts of baby grass blades poke out from the dark moist earth, and sing of springtime. As the child's entire world awakens from its slumber, she rubs the sleep from her eyes, and looks all about her. She stretches her arms above her head and washes herself in the morning sunshine; it is then she notices that her arms and legs have outgrown her clothes. When did she grow? Could it have been while she was sleeping?*

The blizzard becomes a fleeting memory in no time, and like I keep saying, regardless of the weather outside, all we ever do is play and have fun, just like the otters in my school science book. Right now, I'm stuffing a satchel with necessities, because I'm going over to Rosemary's to spend the night. I can hardly wait--it promises to be a very entertaining evening.

When I knock at the Cleeves' kitchen door, Rosemary opens it and greets me, "Hi, Debbie! Come in, come in!"

"Hi, Rosemary, can you believe it that I get to spend the night with you?"

"I guess I do believe it, because here you are!" she says, giggling. Rosemary is always giggling about something or other, and that's why we're such good friends.

The second the layers of my outside gear are peeled off, we traipse into her bedroom to play. Caroline is in the room, though, because they have to share, like Becky and me. While my eyes roam about the room, which is cluttered and jumbled with toys and games, Rosemary attempts a *coup d'état*.

"Caroline, go play somewhere else besides here, okay?"

"No. I want to play with you guys," Caroline whines. She is a master whiner.

"Well, you cannot. So go away," my friend repeats, no gentleness apparent.

"No, no, no!" It seems to me that Caroline has a forceful voice for such a little kid.

"Okay. I'm telling on you. Mom! Caroline won't leave us alone! We're trying to play, and she just keeps getting right in our way!" Rosemary hollers out at the top of her lungs.

Ann Cleeves enters the room and looks things over before she asks, "Rosie, what is it that you and Debbie are doing that can't include your sister?"

"Mom! Please make her go away and leave us alone! She's such a little brat!"

"Now, Dear, she is not a brat. Let her stay and play with you for just a little while, and then I'll ask her to leave you alone, okay?" She smiles sweetly at us and vanishes.

Well, Rosemary is thoroughly incited that her mom won't oblige us by aiding with our attempted take over. So we obviously have to resort to subterfuge. We begin by devising a very secret signal: with fingers crossed, we thrust our hands above our heads, which means to communicate using our secret code. However, possessing no such a code leaves us relying on pretense; we can sure depend on nature's pecking order to aid us, as we relentlessly tease poor Caroline, who's observing us very, very closely. Goody.

"Hugga, bugga booga," Rosemary chants, picking up a raggedy doll, and shaking it in the air.

"Looly, sa booly," I return, taking the doll from her, and hugging it fiercely.

"Ugg, la la toopa," she declares, grinning widely, showing her deep cheek dimples.

"Ooo! Raah, jabbula looly?" I ask, feigning worry and distress.

"Ya, ya! Oooly!" Rosemary answers, clapping her hands happily.

After some time, we are finally rewarded as Caroline abruptly collects a coloring book and a box of crayons, and leaves the room. Ha! Ha! Ha!

"Aren't we clever, Debbie? We sure did fool the little shrimp, huh?"

"Uh-huh." And then, casually inspecting the cluttered room, I wonder, "What should we play next, Rosemary? Have an ideas?" Nothing looks particularly promising from what I'm able to observe.

"I don't know. What do you want to play? How about 'Old Maid'? Or . . . Hey, I know! Maybe we could pretend that we're glamorous Hollywood stars!"

While inspecting the jumble of books in a corner bookshelf, I agree to this suggestion. "Okay. That sounds fun. Do you have any fancy, sparkly dresses?"

"Huh-uh."

"Oh, well." I sigh, becoming bored and disheartened with our sorely lacking inspiration. "Maybe we can watch TV."

"Okay. Let's." She flips on the television and we agree on the "Your Hit Parade" singing program. We sit together on the couch, contented.

"Mom, where is everybody?" she asks, when Mrs. Cleeves glides through the living room with a stack of folded laundry.

"Your dad took the younger children down to the Commissary for a treat. They should be back soon."

"What? Don't I get to have a treat, too, and my friend?" Rosemary is an accomplished whiner; in fact, I think she maybe taught her sister this talent. "Humph!"

Presently, in troop the little kids, flooding the room with incredible amounts of noise and commotion.

Mr. Cleeves settles everyone down, then good-naturedly displays a giant Hershey bar. He breaks off rows of squares and hands them all around; when he sees he has a few squares left over, he offers them to me, because I'm company!

Well, Rosemary insists that this is unfair and grumps, "Humph! Humph!"

While savoring the last of the chocolate, I admire the fact that my friend has crafted humphing down to such a fine art.

Right after breakfast, I announce that I'd promised my mom I'd be home directly, so that I won't wear out my welcome. Rosemary waves to me from the door as I'm off. I'm thankful that she has such a sweet nature, and carries no grudges regarding my windfall from the previous night.

On the way home I spontaneously detour to the playground swings in order to find out whether or not the snow has melted significantly enough to free the swings. Yes! At least, it appears so from this distance.

Negotiating a field of melting spring snow is hazardous; the trick is to remain on top of the hard crust, and not sink into a soft patch.

Finally reaching the swings with no mishaps, I realize that one must stand erect on the seat to pump, as too much snow underneath inhibits sitting down to swing my legs. So, standing on the swing seat, I pump myself to a considerable height; and then, I recklessly bail out, as far as I can, over the snowfield.

"Ouch, ouch, ouch! Owie, my leg!" My jump has rocketed me into a sizeable snow covered boulder. Because of this reckless accident, I must strain and struggle toward my house like a crippled woodland creature, crawling and dragging my injured leg, while hoping that a soft snow patch won't suck me down before reaching safety. My leg hurts awfully, but I rarely cry when I'm hurt, just at any other time, I guess.

Encountering no dilemmas with soft snow patches along the way, I'm finally able to hobble into the house.

"What in the world have you done to yourself, Debbie?" Mom demands, seeing me sprawled out on the utility room floor.

"I've hurt my leg!" I snivel, clutching my shin.

Mom examines my leg, and decides immediately that I need to be seen by a doctor. But even though it's Saturday, Dad is working an extra shift and he's unavailable to drive us. This means that Mom must contact the guards at the gatehouse, and request transportation down to the hospital.

Presently, two guards knock at the door, Officers Bill Peeper and Darrel Stewart. Mr. Stewart carries me out to the station wagon--it does not instantly register in my mind that this vehicle is one of the infamous paddy wagons, as my head is gauzy with mild shock.

Once deposited in an emergency room, Dr. Lindus orders x-rays that confirm a double fracture of my right tibia. He calls a nurse to assist him, and they spend an interminable amount of time wrapping my leg with malodorous, wet, clammy, cold plaster. When the cast has sufficiently dried and set, Mom tells the waiting guards that they can now drive us back up the hill.

--I mentioned earlier that one of the services provided by the Protection Department was to serve as an ambulance, and to be available to provide emergency transportation to residents, free of charge. This happens to be but one more instance of how this group of men made life uncomplicated and stress-free for people in Climax.—

Later Mom arranges a comfortable bed for me in Dad's green recliner chair, as the doctor's instructions were to keep my leg elevated, so that the swelling would lessen. As soon as I'm settled, Mom brings me a late lunch. It doesn't take long for my ego to inflate, because she serves me on one of her brand new TV trays that was a recent Christmas gift; and then Becky and Artie award me with a preview of my unforeseen celebrity status by goggling over my cast, and providing me with all manner of amusements. For these reasons, a broken leg seems a small price to pay for such a plethora of attention.

My mishap has accelerated Mom's resolve to practice her driving, so she and Dad spend some hours in the yellow Olds on Sunday with her behind the wheel. Monday morning dawns with overcast skies, and even though she's not confident enough to drive on snowy roads, in springtime, the streets and roads are just mushy mud. So Mom gathers her courage and drives me to school.

"Mom, you were amazing at driving the car, and I am so glad!" I gush, and smile widely.

"Oh, I guess when push comes to shove, people do more than they imagine they're capable of. And now that I've done it, I really can't imagine why I've held back for so long." She sighs, as she helps me to negotiate the stairs into the school building.

School on this day results in further confirming lofty feelings of regality in my eight-year-old mind. First, Mrs. Ross tells Phillip Cox and Gary Ohmert to move their desks nearer to the windows, so that I can elevate my leg on the extra classroom chair. Before we tackle any geography or arithmetic, I am invited to recount the details of my accident, and I do so with mounds of drama and embellishment. Following my vivid report, Mrs. Ross says that anyone who wants to look at my cast up close may do so. And, beyond this, I have the pleasure of allowing my classmates to help me in a variety of ways throughout the day.

But alas, by midweek, the limelight has faded to a dim flicker, as the novelty of my cast, along with my tiring self-importance, has resulted in a swift fall from glory and I'm now stuck with the reality of an unwieldy encumbrance. Mom has to continue driving me to school, too, for another week and a half, until I can exchange this cast and crutches for a walking cast. I am not at all cheerful during this time.

On an early April Saturday, Artie and his friends, Joe and David, are skiing on the icy springtime snow hill in back of our houses, when Artie falls hard into a tangle of skis and poles. Mom has to drive him down to the emergency room at the hospital. Come to find out he has broken his leg, too!

So, when they get back home with Artie in a cast from hip to toe, Mom says that now my brother must have the recliner chair, which doesn't seem so good to me, handing over a symbol of status and honor, but, since my leg doesn't hurt at all anymore, I step down. And anyway, I have not been allowed TV-tray service at mealtimes for several days, so where is the glory in being delegated use of that chair?

At breakfast on the following Saturday, Mom says to me, "I have a Hi-Homemakers Club meeting today, but it's only going to be an hour long." It appears that Artie and I will be getting the run of the house, a definite first, because Becky will be at a Girl Scout meeting, and Dad is helping Warren Shriver and some other men figure out how to get the boat outside that he's been building in his house all winter.

Well, anyway, Artie has to use crutches—which he has trouble with--for some time longer, before Dr. Lindus can trade it for a walking cast, like the one I have on my leg. Just after Mom dresses for her meeting, she comes into my bedroom and sits on my bed while she finishes fixing her fingernails.

"Debbie, be a good girl and fix your brother some lunch, okay? I'm late as it is." Leaving my room she turns back, and asks, "Are you sure you kids will be all right by yourselves for this little while?"

"Oh, yes, Mom, we absolutely will be fine. And I will fix Artie's lunch, so don't be one bit concerned about us," I declare, and then she whisks out the door.

--Just recently I found a scrap of paper in a storage box that came from my parents' house when it was sold. There was a message written on the yellowed paper that my mother for some reason had saved for all those years. And herein lies the tale of that long ago day:

Box 522
Climax,Colo.
April 41, 1956
Dear Mother,
    *Arthur is being a bad boy. I wanted to fix lunch. But Arthur will not let me. Know he is crying. He is a big baby I think. Don't you think he is.*

                                            *With love,*
                                            *Debbie--*

We've been using our shortcut path both going to and coming home from school for some springtime weeks. We have to be very cautious and stay directly on the pathway, or we'll sink down into deep snow on either edge, and likely get stuck. As a matter of fact, I am agile and adept at staying on the path, even with my walking cast. We can stay outside later, too, because it isn't getting dark quite so early now, and a number of days have actually been warmer. But, in spite of all the signs of spring, Mom insists on us wearing mittens and boots to school, in case there's suddenly a spring snowstorm, which is not unheard of, by any means.

Well, I don't happen to fancy the mittens that I am made to wear. Mom never buys mittens at a store; she designs them and sews them on the machine. She devotes a good deal of time and patience to make sure her efforts yield a quality product, and for the most part, they are nice, and for certain they're amply warm. Mom uses a meticulous process, which she starts by tracing around my hand on a paper to use as a pattern, then uses the pattern of my hand to cut out layers of material, old blankets and sweaters for inside liners, and old denim jeans for the outside cover, and then she sews the entire thing together. The mittens truly are handsome enough, but they possess one feature that just embarrasses me to death: the gigantic thumbs. The finished products always result in mittens with oversized thumbs, so considerable, in fact, that when my hands are inside the mittens I can fold the thumb parts over double.

One springtime day before my friends and I head out for home after school, I ask that they wait for me a minute on the school steps, and then I scramble up to the back of the school that abuts the steep hill, where the ice has melted into a colossal abyss. Once up there, I balance precariously against the ice wall, lean way out over the edge and drop my mittens, watching as they float, like lifeless birds, down into the icy, blue-water pond. Days later, when my mom wonders what's become of my mittens, I simply tell her that they've mysteriously disappeared--this is a little white lie, I guess . . . or then again, maybe one worthy of the confessional.

At long last, the day arrives for my cast to be removed. When Dr. Lindus cuts the last bit with the menacing saw, freeing me, I inspect my frightfully shrunken leg and stare with consternation at the pinkish, fish-scaly skin. Once emancipated from the cast, I don't even mind wearing my red rubber boots that are challenging to get on and off, because the soft lining is almost always damp from snow that has gotten inside from the top and melted. More often than not, while taking them off, my foot nips out with my shoe remaining inside the boot.

On an afternoon in early May, I'm walking home from school alone on the path because Rosemary sometimes leaves me at 8th Street, so that she can get to her house sooner. I pause to stare at a winking, shiny object in the middle of the vast snowfield. Overcome by a burning desire to discover what it is, and sensing that it may be a precious treasure, I take a deep breath and step from the hardened path. Tiptoeing along with extreme caution, ever so slowly and gingerly, I'm feeling lucky, because, so far, I've managed to remain on top of the hard snow crust. But, just as I progress to within a mere couple of feet of the treasure, or whatever it is, here comes my nemesis, Jimmy Ducharme, larking along the path on his way home from school.

Cupping his hands around his mouth, he taunts, "Hey, Debbie, don't get stranded way out there, or you might end up a frozen cry baby!"

"Sticks and stones can break my bones, but names can never hurt me!" I shout, practicing my fearless, plucky voice on him.

"Okay, smarty-pants. See how you like this!" he bellows, and starts pummeling me with icy snowballs. Some of them naturally hit the mark—me--which absolutely infuriates me.

"You are the meanest, most wretched boy in camp, and I'm telling on you!" I barrel over the snow as fast as I can, in a futile attempt to speed past him up to 9th Street, and then race home ahead of him to tell. But this mindless challenge is the instant source of my demise, when my leg sinks down into the deep snow and stops me short. I twist and jerk and struggle for all I'm worth, but I am stuck like a rabbit with its foot pinned in a steel trap!

"You'd better come over here and help get me out, Jimmy, or I really will tell on you!" I suck back my tears, despairing inwardly that crying, like I always do, will likely accelerate his hostility toward me.

"Ho! Who cares?" And he sets off, nonchalantly, leaving me there, stuck fast!

Well, there's nothing for it but to keep straining and exerting to free my leg that's stuck deep in the snow way above my knee, almost up to my middle. I'm not wearing snow pants, and since I always wear a dress to school, my bare leg throbs and stings from being scratched and scraped with icy snow crust. For a while, I attempt to banish thoughts of bleeding to death from my leg injuries, and instead concentrate and survey the path, willing *any* kid to materialize and rescue me. I wait and wish, mightily. Nobody.

An interminable amount of time passes with my leg stuck deep in this cavity, when I get a considerable surprise: Jimmy returns with Artie and Jacky in tow! Well, I am struck dumb, and shake my head back and forth, and blink rapidly to convince myself that I'm not imagining things.

"Hey, Debbie. Don't worry. We'll get you out of there," Artie says, still with a walking cast on his leg.

The trio sets out across the field in a slow crawl, but then we all hear an ominous rumbling that portends melting activity under the snow. They drop onto their bellies and inch along with additional carefulness, my brother dragging his encumbered leg.

"Yeah. Just hold on until we get over to you," Jimmy says, a trifle unnecessarily as I don't see myself suddenly rising like a zephyr, unaided.

Upon reaching me, all three jabber directions as to what I should do. I pull fiercely on my leg, while twisting and turning my foot. And then they all grasp hold of my arms and start tugging on me. But I stay stuck.

"Try to move your foot around inside your boot down in there," Jimmy coaches me. "And, at the same time, we'll keep pulling on your arms."

I hold back any sarcastic remarks, and instead, work with concentrated effort and renewed energy for some more minutes, until finally . . . out pops my leg with a swoosh and suction release, shoeless and bootless, but never mind. Each of them shows concern, along with a morbid appreciation, when they inspect the rainbow colors on my scraped and bleeding leg. I, myself, am considerably impressed by the extent of damage the crystalline snow was capable of causing.

As soon as I'm on top once more, I peer down into the minor chasm where I've been stuck, and attempt to see to the bottom, but all I'm able to discern is icy blue water--no boot. We each take a turn while lying flat on the snow to see if we can get the boot back, but after several attempts, we agree that the boot and shoe are not recoverable. And so, in a moderate state of anguish, I limp along with the others, wearing only a soggy sock on my foot.

"Hope you don't get in too much trouble for losing your boot and shoe, Debbie," Jimmy says, heading for his house with his brother.

"Thanks for helping to get me unstuck, Jimmy. 'Bye." And I stand motionless, ruminating over the unimaginable events of the past hour and a half. "Now, why in the world is Jimmy being so nice to me?" I just cannot rationalize it.

"You're probably going to be in trouble for losing your shoe and boot," Artie warns with concern, as he plunks along the driveway.

Which slams me back to reality in a flash. My head is swimming with miserable scenarios, and the inevitable tears start streaming, so that by the time I move toward the kitchen door with Artie, I am verging on histrionics.

Mom's at the stove frying pork chops; she turns instantly and asks in alarm, "What's the matter, Debbie? Did you hurt yourself?"

"No." And then, between sobs and hiccoughs, "I mean, yes, I did hurt my leg, because I got stuck deep in the snow by the path, and I lost my boot with my shoe in it."

All in all, the whole incident was not given much importance, other than my being lectured on responsible behavior, and, naturally, the wasteful need to replace snow boots at the end of a season.

Later on in May, I must stay home from school for a couple of days because I've caught a cold and cough along with a mild case of measles. I've been taking an afternoon nap, when I hear voices outside. Kids are home from school and its very sunny and almost balmy outside. I gaze longingly from my bedroom window at the street scene, where I can see that everybody is playing, floating boats and making dams in the muddy streams of snow melt. My desire to join in the fun swells to a crescendo.

Impulsively, I shrug into my robe, slip on my slippers, and creep through the house—ha, I don't see my mom in any of the usual places. Well, before I realize how or what I'm doing, I've joined the splashing and laughing 10th Street kids in the muddy street. But, before long, Dad comes along from work; as he drives by slowly and notices me, he gestures for me to get myself into the house. I'm instantly doused with dread, like an ill-fated critter at the edge of a busy highway.

Dad turns from the kitchen sink where he's rinsing out his thermos when I come slopping into the kitchen in my wet, muddy slippers.

"Deborah! Get those wet things off, and go into the bedroom and wait for me!" Dad commands, shortly, in a stern voice, and with annoyance showing in his eyes. The way he emphasizes my name speaks volumes; he only calls me Deborah when he's dismayed with my complete lack of good sense.

I trudge slowly along the hallway and into Mom and Dad's bedroom, there to await my misfortune. My stomach is full of frenzied, shameful quivers that extend deep, deep down into my insides. I realize that I've been caught in a foolhardy activity, and that my dad must discipline me. I also grasp the certainty that no one can rescue me, or even plead insanity in my defense. Not Becky, not anyone . . . I face this alone.

At long last, Dad crosses the threshold to do his duty, and to remind me that if I choose to misbehave, I must endure the consequences. Jeepers!

But maybe this particular misadventure was ultimately worth it because it sure was fun splashing in the cold, yellowish water that had melted from snows high on the ridges of Mt. Bartlett. Sniffling out of the bedroom and down the hallway, I study the dried mud on my arm; it's easy to extend my imagination, and presume that some of it slid right off the hogback, someplace near Phillipson's grave, maybe. I can just hardly wait for summer to be here again!

# Chapter Fifteen

*"Nothing lasts forever." "Time marches on." "Out with the old, in with the new."*
*"Nothing can stand in the way of progress." "All good things must come to an*
*end." Each of these becomes a trite axiom, when used in reference to a young girl's*
*precious memories of a mining town that mixed a rare metal with ordinary mud*
*and used it to sculpt its young people into works of art.*

--In January, 1958, the Climax Molybdenum Company merged with the American Metals Corporation and became a division called American Metals Climax, Inc., or AMAX. It soon became apparent to the east coast home-based Corporation that the Climax community was in the way of the mine and mill's further development and expansion.

After several months of study and consideration, a decision was made to move the camp lock, stock, and barrel down the hill thirteen miles to Leadville. AMAX purchased a large tract of land just to the north of Leadville's city limits, and contracted with a Colorado Springs developer, American Builders, Inc., to construct several hundred new homes in a modern Levittown-style subdivision, called West Park. However, because of a Climax union strike in the late fall of '58, only a hundred of the new homes were completed, and of these, a mere twenty-eight had been sold and were being occupied.

The strike didn't last long, only six weeks, but it took its toll on both the Company and the union. Hundreds of miners packed up their families and moved to other places, not knowing that it wouldn't take long before a labor agreement would be reached.

In the meantime, the Company had hired a "company town mover," the J.W. Galbreath Company, to move all of the houses and community buildings from Climax to West Park. Highway 91 from Climax to Leadville was an absolute spectacle to behold from August 1960 through September 1962 as flatbed trucks moved house after house down the mountainside, along with big old cumbersome buildings. The eighteen-unit apartment buildings were cut into three sections, and then placed on the flatbeds. Traffic on the highway had to be stopped for hours each day, so that these wide loads could maneuver through the curves.

The only structures left in camp were those needed by the Company for office buildings, and the Fremont Trading Company, which remained doing business at the summit of Fremont Pass for several more years. Oh, and the guardhouse, of course, because the Company required the Protection Department to remain on the premises.

My family moved to Leadville in the fall of 1958. I was ten and entering the fifth grade, and much too young at that time to feel nostalgic for a hometown which only later would provide such a wealth of rich memories. As for leaving my friends behind, well, I knew that before much time passed, they too would be moving to Leadville. Although some of us Climax kids went to the Catholic parochial school, St. Mary's, at 9th and Hemlock, including the Ducharme boys, the overall majority went to the Leadville public schools. And, as a matter of fact, for a few months while the construction on our houses was being completed, we shared a car pool with the Ducharmes, and so my adversary--whose soft heart was known to surface at times--lived nearby for a few years, until the time came when his family moved away from Leadville, for good.

When the Max Schott School closed its doors forever in June of 1960, the last of the Climax kids had to endure a forced merger with the students in Leadville. Because the two high schools had been basketball rivals during decades past, the transition for the older kids proved to be interesting. Briefly, there were skirmishes and exchanges of insults among some of the juniors and seniors, but for the most part, the joining of the two high schools turned out to be relatively painless.

During the '70's, the Company started the open-pit mining process that caused most of the summit of Mt. Bartlett to collapse, and, along with the mountaintop, our icon, the Glory Hole, vanished. In the early '80s, the Climax Molybdenum Division of AMAX began to spiral into a downward slide that was precipitated by a collapsing molybdenum world market, which happens to be a gross over-simplification of the circumstances.

The mine stayed open but continued to decline in output and laid off employees throughout the '90s, until, finally, today there remains but a skeletal staff left with the responsibility of maintaining the upkeep of the property, and of the continuing reclamation of land and water. It was during the '50s that the government mandated that monies be accrued and kept in an escrow account by the Corporation for the eventual and inevitable reclamation of the Climax property. The funds in escrow grew substantially throughout the years, making possible the ongoing projects at Climax; these are among the most successful mining reclamations in the nation.

As for all the kids mentioned in the narrative, in addition to the Ducharme brothers, Bobbie Middleton, Rosemary Cleeves, Evelyn, Danny and David Prier, Ava Lou, Bonnie, David, and Mike Brothers, Catherine, Mary, Patrick and Joe Wadsworth, Danny McAuliff and Rusty Brewer, all went to school in Leadville; and, given the feisty spirit of this group, who would be surprised to see any of them snub their nose at life's adversities? And, given the collective personality that these Climax kids possessed, would it be such a marvel if they overcame the world? The Climax kids made sure it worked.

And thus, a town found a new address; but it is because of the spirit of the hardy residents that the heart and soul of Climax will live on forever in the stories told by grandparents and great-grandparents. It is for our progeny that the history of Climax must be set down on paper, so that a remarkable people and place not be lost in time.

Interestingly enough, the guardhouse--always a sentinel of sorts-- remains yet today in the very location where it once did when I was a little girl. And indeed, it may very well be keeping watch over the ghost of Mt Bartlett with its Glory Hole and its spectacular surroundings.—

*Author's Brownie Troop. Author kneeling far left; Rosemary Cleeves kneeling second from left.*

*Author, far right*

*Author's First Communion*

*The Vincent Family in Climax*

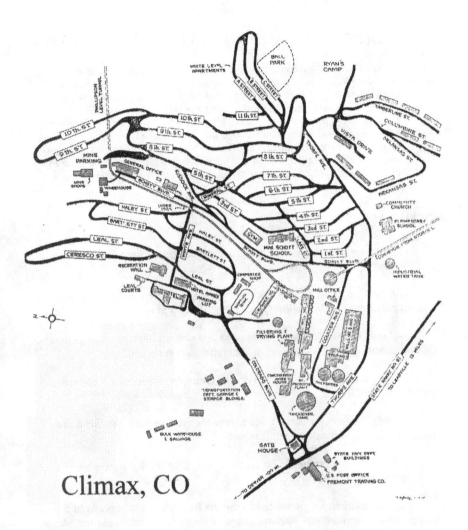

## Climax, CO

# COMMUNITY RULES AND REGULATIONS          1956

In operating a self-governed town most anywhere in our country, an elected government will adopt a set of ordinances designed to give the people of the town rules and regulations which serve the best interests of all. The rules and regulations presented in this pamphlet have been adopted for this very same reason.

Since the entire community of Climax is located on private (company) property, we have our own community protection department to safeguard our residents, to see that regulations are complied with and to offer every assistance to residents and visitors. If you have a question or problem regarding these rules and regulations, we sincerely invite you to contact a protection officer or call the community manager's office.

## GENERAL

Employees must have their identification badges on their person while on company property.

All persons, other than employees, entering camp must stop and obtain a written pass from the Protection Office in the Reception enter.

All visitors in industrial areas must have a written pass from the General Office to show Protection Officers or supervisors upon request.

The use of firearms or the carrying of concealed weapons on company premises is forbidden.

Residents having pets must not permit them to become a public nuisance. All dogs must be vaccinated against rabies.

All school children are to be off the streets after the 9 p.m. curfew, unless accompanied by an adult.

School children are permitted to use the Recreation Hall only until 5 p.m. except when organized activities are available to them. Children are not allowed to use the Recreation Hall on Sundays.

Skiing or sledding on the streets is forbidden.

Disorderly or unlawful conduct is not permitted on company premises.

All guests at the hotel must abide by the regulations established by the hotel management.

# Afterword

Celia Vincent died in 1989, succumbing to cancer after a valiant fight of several years.

Becky Vincent Kirk died in 1993 of brain cancer.
(They each hugely influenced and provoked this endeavor, from beyond their graves.)

Art Vincent is retired in Lakewood, CO, sees his Climax mine buddies regularly, and never shovels snow.

Art, Jr., with a degree in geology, works on rocket fuels, and lives with his wife, Ricki, in Lakewood, CO.

Rusty Brewer is the author's former spouse and the father of their two grown daughters.

Rosemary Cleeves and her husband, Ken Curry, were witnesses at the author's second marriage.

Jimmy Ducharme, wherever you are, please understand and appreciate the literary license I took with your character!

# SOURCES

<u>Moly Mountain News</u>

| | |
|---|---|
| 6/15/53 | early history – Climax is named |
| 1/25/54 | guard stories |
| 7/27/53 | picture story of Glory Hole |
| 9/21/53 | health care costs |
| 5/23/64 | Coyote Blast |
| 3/64 | short history of the mine & mill |
| 4/11/52 | Blue Devils champs |

5/23/54    <u>Denver Post Empire Magazine</u>

This is Climax Molybdenum – public relations brochure (1979)

"Timberline" Max Schott School yearbooks (1953, 54, 55, 56, 57)

KEZW radio station 14.30 AM Denver

<u>CO Law Magazine</u> (August, 1960)

## *Personal Interviews*

| | |
|---|---|
| Rusty Brewer | 8/02 |
| "Flash" Gordon | 8/02 |
| James J Ludwig | 8/02 |
| Dan McAuliffe | 8/03 |
| Sharon Shriver | 7/03 |
| Darrell Stewart | 8/02 |
| Howard Tritz | 8/02 |
| C.T. Trevethan | 8/02 |
| Arthur L Vincent | 6/02-03 |

Jim & Irene Witmer     7/02

2/54    Climax Telephone Directory

# About the Author

D.E. Vincent loves traveling, camping, and playing poker. She spends her leisure time occupied with her grandchildren. Vincent has taught English Language Arts, Drama, and Reading in Middle School for twenty years in Southwest Denver, Colorado. She lives with her husband in the Denver foothills.

CPSIA information can be obtained
at www.ICGtesting.com
Printed in the USA
FSHW011324180221